MW00379083

The Rider's Guide To Real Collection

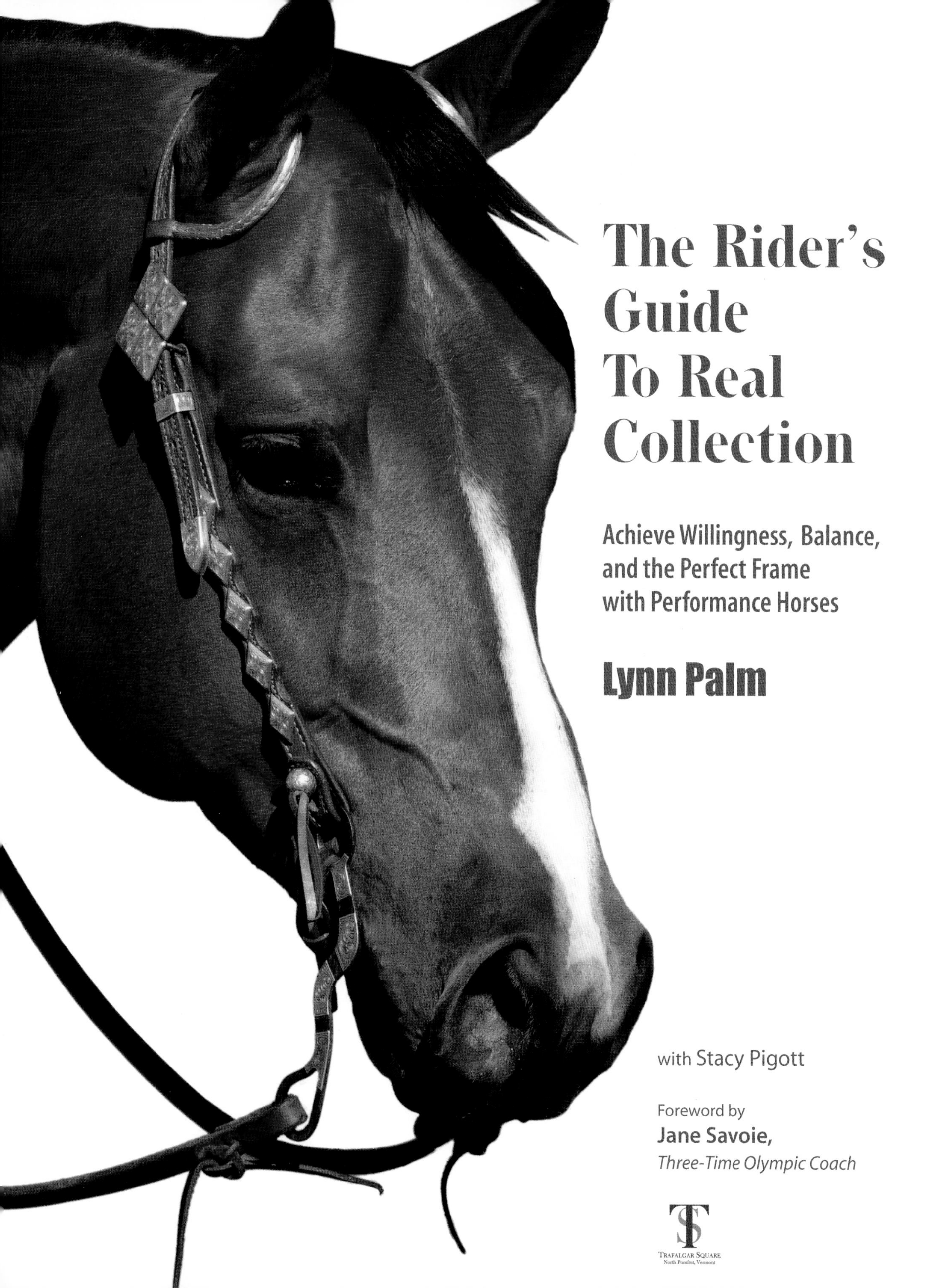

The Rider's Guide To Real Collection

Achieve Willingness, Balance, and the Perfect Frame with Performance Horses

Lynn Palm

with Stacy Pigott

Foreword by
Jane Savoie,
Three-Time Olympic Coach

TS
TRAFALGAR SQUARE
North Pomfret, Vermont

First published in 2010 by
Trafalgar Square Books
North Pomfret, Vermont 05053

Printed in China

Library of Congress Cataloging-in-Publication Data

Palm, Lynn.
The rider's guide to real collection : achieve willingness, balance, and the perfect frame with performance horses / Lynn Palm with Stacy Pigott.
p. cm.
Includes index.
ISBN 978-1-57076-444-8
1. Horses--Training. I. Pigott, Stacy. II. Title.
SF287.P35 2010
636.1'0835--dc22
2010019917

All photos by Cappy Jackson except: figs. 1.6, 2.6, 5.2 A–D, 5.3 A & B, 5.4 A–C, 5.6, and 9.7 by Stacy Pigott; figs. 3.5 A & B, 3.6, 3.8 A–D, 3.9, and 9.17 A–C by Cyril Pittion-Rossillon; fig. 3.7 by Sarah Gentry; fig. 4.6 by Billie Lewis; fig. 6.3 by Neal Bro; fig. 7.6 A by Kat Rogers

Illustrations by Cyril Pittion-Rossillon except fig. 7.5 B from the book *Reining Essentials* by Sandy Collier with Jennifer Forsberg Meyer

Book design by Carrie Fradkin
Cover design by RM Didier
Typefaces: Myriad MM, Impact

10 9 8 7 6 5 4 3 2 1

Dedication

To my best friend and husband Cyril Pittion-Rossillon, who has been my partner in training horses and teaching students for more than two decades. Our dressage foundations and shared goals have allowed us to develop unique, "easy to achieve and understand" training methods based on dressage principles. I love sharing our passion for the horse together, and passing on our knowledge to horse lovers who want to have happy and willing horses in everything they do.

And to my mentor, the late Bobbi Steele, who gave me the education, inspiration, and confidence to pursue an equestrian career. She taught me to be an outstanding rider who always asked and understood the "why" behind every action. She instilled in me the belief that dressage is for all breeds of horses and any riding discipline. Ms. Steele gave me the tools to train with understanding, allowing me to build trust and educate the horse naturally, whether the intent is competition or recreation.

Contents

Foreword by Jane Savoie

I was delighted and honored when Lynn Palm asked me if I would write the foreword for her new book on the often misunderstood and confusing topic of collection.

Before I tell you a bit about the book, I have to say something about Lynn. I've known her for many years as a trainer, student, and performer. Lynn is truly the consummate horsewoman. She never ceases to amaze me with her knowledge, experience, and insight into the mind of both horses and riders.

Lynn's been teaching and training for a long time, yet she's always interested in learning and growing. She's an accomplished and decorated champion, yet she's always humble. Above all, she keeps the well-being and happiness of her horses uppermost in her mind throughout her training. And, although she takes training seriously, she always keeps learning fun...and isn't that why we all got into riding in the first place?

I particularly love how she just "gets it." So many professionals put themselves in isolated catagories and declare, "I'm a jumper rider," or "I'm a reiner," or "I'm a dressage rider." Unlike many of us who specialize in just one area of training, Lynn is, indeed, the ultimate trainer for all riders in every equestrian discipline. She understands that good training is just *good training*. She uses basic dressage principles as the foundation for all her work. From that solid foundation, horses and riders can go on to specialize successfully in any type of riding.

In *The Rider's Guide to Real Collection*, Lynn explains the what, why, and "how to" of teaching your horse to collect. She also discusses a number of factors that affect a horse's ability to shift his weight back and lighten the forehand. And probably most importantly, she explains the ingredients that go into laying the correct foundation to achieve *true* collection so you don't resort to shortcuts that only create an artificial headset.

Although the primary focus of the book is collection, Lynn leaves no stone unturned. She covers everything from ground training equipment to proper tack to fun exercises that will keep you on the right path throughout the various stages of achieving the end goal of collection. I'm sure you'll love *The Rider's Guide to Real Collection* as much as I did. All in all, you'll find it chock full of informative, easy-to-digest riding theory and practical exercises. So pull on your boots, and enjoy the ride!

Jane Savoie
Three-Time Olympic Coach, Author, and
Alternate for the US Olympic Dressage Team

Acknowledgments

THANKS FROM LYNN

There are so many people who have made this book possible. It is impossible to thank everyone, although there are a few special people I would like to mention.

Stacy Pigott: From the first time I spoke with you on the phone I knew we could work together, and after nearly a year of writing magazine articles with you about training horses to collect, I knew you were the one to write this book for me. The best part is you grew up showing all-around pleasure horses in Michigan and had watched me compete for years, so you knew what I was saying about collection from the start. I know that your wonderful talent with words and knowledge of horses helps make the language of my methods easy to understand. Thanks to Trafalgar Square for accepting you as my writer, even though this was your first book. I do hope that this one will bring us together for another in the future, and that you also have the opportunity to write other books because of this experience.

Cappy Jackson: You are an all-around great person: fun, unbelievably talented, and amazing to work with. You always capture the very best in a horse, whether standing or in motion, and whatever the discipline. I have had wonderful experiences working with you on shoots for magazine articles and books over the years. (On this one alone, we did over 4,000 pictures in one day!) Thank you for being a special friend and educating people through your beautiful photos.

Heidi Burkhalter: You and your wonderful husband Walter are very special clients and friends. You have given me such support and trust as we shared successful show horses together, as well as so many positive days of life!

Carol Harris: You are a great horsewoman and my mentor. I will always cherish your friendship and incredible wisdom, as well as the business relationship we share. From the first horse you sent to me in 1973, Rugged Cash, to the beautiful 16-year relationship with your famous Quarter Horse Stallion, Rugged Lark, you and your horses are always in my heart. Thank you for the many opportunities you have given me, trusting me to "bring out the best" in the horses you breed.

Jane Savoie: I love and appreciate your understanding that dressage is for everyone. You are such a talented educator and a dynamic trainer; I always relish the opportunity to ride and train with you. Ms. Bobbi Steele taught me, "If you think you know all about horses, you will always stay at one level." You are the perfect example of someone who never stops learning and always strives to be at the top, doing the best you can for horses and riders!

Al Dunning: You are my favorite horseman in the Western horse world. Since our friendship started in the early 1970s, we have always respected each other's talents and shared our knowledge. The training DVD we produced in 2009, *Western Dressage*, is one of my favorite educational pieces to show the similarities in training a reining horse and a hunter horse, using dressage principles. Thank you, and your talented wife Becky, for the opportunity to share so much over the years!

William Sweeny, DVM, and Gene Thomas, DVM: Both of you have imparted so much knowledge about horse care, medicating and healing horses, and producing healthy, fit horses for the show ring. You taught me to maintain show horses without drugs and to keep my horses naturally fit and sound. You are truly team players who, along with open-minded blacksmiths, have allowed me to succeed in training my horses and competing in the show ring.

Sandy Collier: I have always appreciated your kind training methods and the way you take your time to make great horses. You have risen above to succeed in two male-dominated events—working cow horse and reining. I will never forget the help you offered with the training of my longtime friend Rugged Painted Lark.

Carla Wennberg: You will always be a special protégé of mine. I loved teaching you as a young girl, and knew you would love dressage. I am so proud to see you take dressage principles and use them to train all-around pleasure horses. As one of the top collegiate equine educators in the country, you are a great inspiration to young equestrians everywhere, and I am very proud of you.

Stephanie Lynn: Many people have worked with me, but you are one of the few who has excelled with your own business. I am proud of your success as a coach of youth and amateur riders, and of the national and World Champion American Quarter Horses you have trained. You are a person I now look up to as a horsewoman and highly-regarded AQHA judge.

Kevin Dukes: Kevin, you, Stephanie, and Carla are my three favorite former employees! You are a fine example of all-around training at its best, training horses with passion and respect. It is easy to see you and your wife Melissa put the horse first, using kind and understanding methods to produce willing horses that perform for a long time.

Marie-Frances Davis: From the first day I saw you ride at one of my clinics, you have shown me how focused and successful young people can be. Your great attitude and determination to succeed were apparent as you completed an internship and started as a stable assistant. Today, as General Manager of Palm Partnership Training and a profit-sharing owner, you have proven to be an invaluable part of the company—capably managing the stable, horses, staff and clients; assisting with training and showing; helping me teach at horse expos; taking care of accounting, sales, and marketing; and even overseeing needed repairs at the farm. Everyone needs a Marie! We are proud that you are such a loyal part of our business.

Anthony and Elizabeth Salvatori—my beloved parents: You were so wonderful to let me chart a path with horses, which you knew nothing about. Dad, when you and I went to Cain's Pony Farm and you bought my first pony, "Sugar" (of course I had to have the one that was pregnant, and we soon had "Honey," too), you changed my life. Your early help with my business (I remember my first brochure, Salvatori School of Horsemanship!) and your willingness to co-sign on loans is what got me started. Mom, I will always remember my "Horse Show Mom" who started the largest 4-H horse club in the state of Florida. From my first horse, "Cracker," who you bought for $150 (including a saddle and bridle!) and who taught me how to take correct leads (as he only had one!) to my second horse "Mocha Dell" (who Mom and I bought while Dad was on a business trip!)—a weanling who'd never been away from home until she was delivered to our house. We put her in the paddock and of course she jumped out immediately! So we used rope to make a higher fence...those were the days—and fabulous memories!

THANKS FROM STACY

To Lynn Palm: You are a talented and amazing woman I have looked up to since my youth days showing pleasure horses in Michigan. I am honored and eternally grateful that you chose me to write your book. You are an inspiration!

To everyone at Trafalgar Square Books: Thank you for taking a chance on this magazine writer! I couldn't ask for a better group of women to mentor me through the process of writing my first book.

To Christie Nissenson and Wendy Furmanek: You both believed in me when I didn't. You gave me the strength to make it through several drafts, the occasional case of writer's block, and countless late-night editing sessions. I could not have done it without either of you. Thank you for always being there for me, and for being you!

Most importantly, to my parents, Larry and Judy Pigott. I owe you an enormous debt of gratitude for the sacrifices you made that allowed me to follow my dreams. You have always been my biggest supporters in everything I do, which has given me the courage to try new things. Mom and Dad, you always said I should write a book; here it is.

What Is Collection?

COLLECTION IS ONE OF THE MOST MISUNDERSTOOD CONCEPTS IN RIDING. EVERYBODY wants it, but few people truly understand how to get it. Fortunately, every horse can achieve and move in a collected frame with time and patience. Learning how to bring the horse into true collection gives you an easy, commonsense understanding of how the horse's anatomy and mechanics naturally work, and how you can improve your horse's performance, create a more willing equine partner, extend his physical and mental longevity, and enjoy the ride even more.

Importance of Collection

When a horse is collected, he is more balanced so it's easier for him to do what he's asked (fig. 1.1). He can change gaits; change speed in gaits; turn; go up and down hills; move laterally; jump; stop; and spin—all with less difficulty.

The horse's movement is more rhythmic, free, and flowing. His walk has a marching, defined pace, where you can shorten or lengthen the stride without losing a four-beat rhythm. The trot has suspension and a precise two-beat rhythm. The canter is a true three-beat gait, where the natural length of stride is elongated and maximized. Collection "magnifies" movements and maximizes the horse's potential.

◀ *1.1* A balanced and collected horse can perform maneuvers with ease.

Collection also gives the rider light and easy control of the horse: he is responsive to his rider and "locked in" to what you are asking him to do. It's almost like a dance—everything is effortless and light. There are differences to the horse's frame in collection for specific riding disciplines and horse breeds, but a *horse in balance* is the same—in all riding. Collected naturally and correctly, he is going to be able to excel in whatever event or competition he is doing. He will be comfortable and relaxed, and certainly more fun to ride.

Definition of True Collection

True collection, also known as the horse being in "self-carriage," is achieved when he is able to compress his body and move in a shorter, "rounded" frame (figs. 1.2 A–C). It starts when a horse engages the joints of his hind legs more and brings them further underneath his body as he moves, allowing him to bear more weight on his hind end. When he does, his hindquarters lower, his back comes up and is "round" rather than flat, and his withers are elevated, thus allowing the front legs to carry less weight. The neck and poll also rise; he "breaks" at the poll; and the head comes on the vertical (see p. 6).

Collection can only be achieved by riding from *back to front*. This means using your driving aids—your seat and legs—before your rein aids, to create a connection from the horse's hind legs to his mouth. The power in the horse's hindquarters is directed forward through his body to your hands. He begins to round his spine and come "on the bit," which is necessary for his future ability to collect. A horse on the bit is properly connected from back to front, which is sometimes referred to as "connected from the leg to the rein"; "moving in a round frame"; "throughness"; "packaged"; or "rounding his back."

Definition of False Collection

A "headset" is not collection (fig. 1.3). This is probably one of the biggest misconceptions in riding. Achieving a headset is *part* of collection, but it's *not* collection. "False collection" is perpetuated through techniques such as overflexion, neck bending, and riding from the mouth. These often result in artificial gaits (see p. 7), a frustrated and resistant horse, and poor performance.

Feel What Your Horse Feels

One of the quickest ways to understand true collection is to try it yourself. First, get on your hands and knees, with your knees directly under your hips and your hands directly under your shoulders (fig. 1.4 A). In this position, you're going to have your head above your back because it's more comfortable. Because of the weight of your head and neck, you're going to feel more weight on your hands

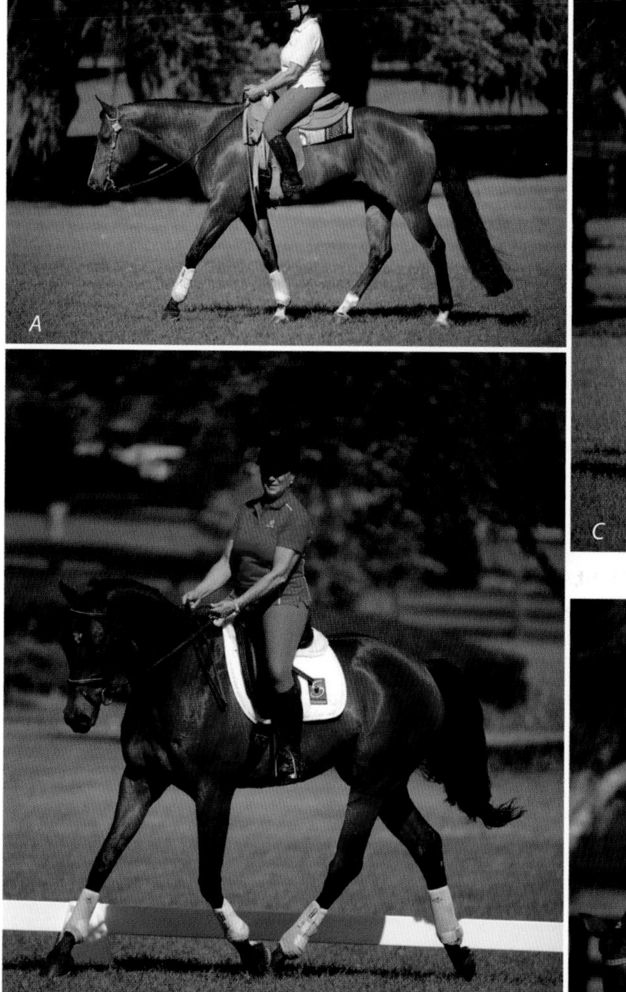

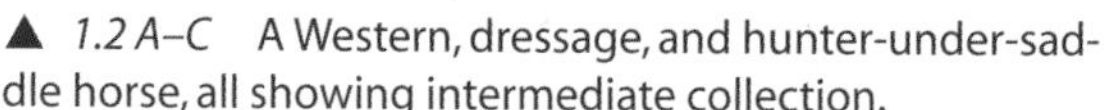
▲ *1.2 A–C* A Western, dressage, and hunter-under-saddle horse, all showing intermediate collection.

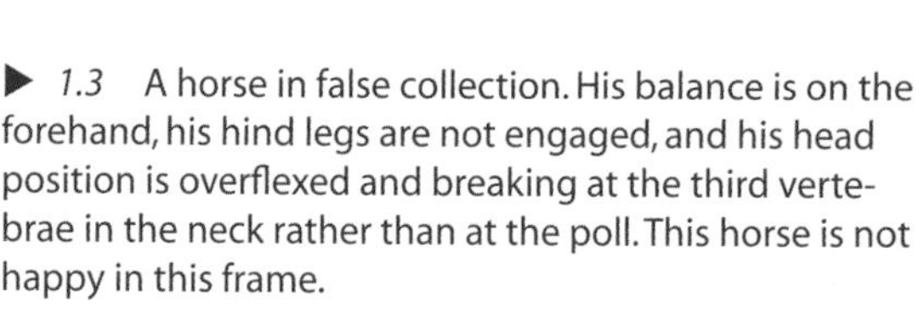
▶ *1.3* A horse in false collection. His balance is on the forehand, his hind legs are not engaged, and his head position is overflexed and breaking at the third vertebrae in the neck rather than at the poll. This horse is not happy in this frame.

▲ *1.4 A–F* Demonstrating natural self carriage (A). With your front and hind "legs" squarely beneath your hips and shoulders, there is enough lightness in your "forehand" to allow for a fairly easy canter depart (B). Next, we demonstrate correct collection (C). When you are correctly collected with your hind "legs" underneath your torso and your back round, more weight is transferred off the forehand, allowing for a very easy canter depart (as in this example) and for more advanced maneuvers (D). Finally, false collection with more weight and balance on the forehand and the head position behind the vertical (E). When your hind "legs" aren't engaged, your back is flat, and more of your weight is on your "forehand," it is not at all easy to do a simple canter depart (F).

than on your knees—the same as the horse in natural carriage. Now, pretend you are doing a canter depart (fig. 1.4 B). You should find that you can bring your hands off the ground without difficulty, although perhaps not as gracefully as you would like.

When collection is achieved through training and developing the horse's body, the hind legs engage and move forward deep underneath his body, the spine rounds, and the forehand elevates. To simulate this, bring your knees underneath yourself to round and elevate your back (fig. 1.4 C). Try your canter depart again. You should be able to lift your hands easily: This position simulates a horse that is collected (fig. 1.4 D).

Next, you're going to "set" your head, like a horse in false collection. Put your head down so it is level with, or below your topline (fig. 1.4 E). You should feel the added weight on your hands at this point. When this happens to the horse, he can't bring his hind legs underneath his body to start collecting himself. Move your knees far behind your hips. Now pick up your canter (fig. 1.4 F). It should be extremely hard to lift your hands off the ground. This is what your horse experiences, too!

My Mentor, Bobbi Steele

I was seven years old when we moved to Sarasota, Florida. A wonderful lady named Bobbi Steele lived down the street, and I would ride my bike over to watch her ride her horses. Finally, one day she stopped, introduced herself, and invited me in. After that, I rode with her for more than 30 years, and my parents never paid for one lesson. She knew I was crazy about horses, and since she was retired, she just took me under her wing.

Ms. Steele was unique and special in her time. She was born in 1908 to an Illinois farming family. Her parents wouldn't let her have a horse so as a teenager she ran away to the circus and was hired as a rider. At the time, Ringling Brothers hired European trainers for their horse acts, so for the next 10 years Ms. Steele rode with German dressage trainer Captain William Hyer.

While she worked for the circus, she developed two horses to do exhibitions on her own: Gay Rhythm did all of the trot work and Night Call, the canter work. As an entertainer she performed at all of the major shows—Madison Square Garden, the American Royal, the Royal Canadian Horse Show, all the best. I have a picture of Night Call, a black Thoroughbred. She would dismount, walk a set distance in front of him, kneel on one knee, and hold a small, round stick over her head. Then, with the horse at liberty and no attachments, she would call to him, and he would jump over her, stop, and face her on the other side.

Ms. Steele's amazing story was featured in an eight-page article entitled "Girl Rider Excels at Rare Type of 18th Century Horsemanship" in the October 14, 1946, issue of LIFE Magazine.

Ms. Steele taught me that if I wanted a horse—no matter what I wanted to do with him—I had to become a good rider. The better I got at what I was doing, the more I would be able to achieve with him. I learned on a three-year-old Saddlebred/Quarter Horse cross that she had named Nic Nack. I rode him for about 12 years. After a lesson, we'd always go into her house, sit down with a Coca-Cola®, and talk about the lesson. She'd explain to me "why" we were doing certain things and what the next stage was. Then, I'd go home and try what I was learning on my own horses. The dressage background she had—and taught me—has enabled me to do what I've done: Her barn was where I really learned to train and teach.

Flexion and Bend

▲ *1.5 A–C* On the vertical (A), beyond the vertical (B), and behind the vertical (C).

When your horse's head position is *on the vertical*, his forehead is at a 90-degree angle to the ground—that is, on a vertical line (fig. 1.5 A). This is the maximum position that a horse should *flex* at the poll. When the nose is further out than 90 degrees to the ground, the horse's head position is considered *beyond the vertical* (fig. 1.5 B). When the nose is straight out and there is no flexion at the poll, there is no roundness to the spine so there can be no collection. This position is sometimes referred to as "nosed out" or it is said that a horse "noses out."

When the nose goes *behind the vertical*, such as when the horse tucks his chin toward his chest, he is flexing at the third vertebrae in the neck and no longer correctly flexing at the poll (fig. 1.5 C). This is known as "overflexing."

Too often, I see riders pull on the reins to get the horse to "give" to the bit and fix the head inward. The first thing this does is restrict the horse from going forward. The only escape the horse has from the pain he feels in his mouth is to lower his head even further and/or behind the vertical. When a horse goes behind the vertical and is overflexed, he has the advantage of escaping the action you are giving with your rein aids to the bit. In other words, if you wanted to turn, he could avoid the cue. And if you wanted to slow down, he could certainly escape by bringing his chin toward his chest. Whenever your horse is overflexed you have a loss of control and usually cannot totally regain correct responses when you need them.

Many people *bend* the horse's neck from *side to side* to try to achieve a headset (fig. 1.6). As said earlier, trying to obtain "collection" from the horse's head and neck only results in a *false* collection. The neck is just one part of the entire body of the horse. I like to divide the horse into five parts: head; neck; shoulder and front legs; back and barrel; hip and hind legs. If your main focal point is bending the neck back and forth and pulling on the mouth constantly, you are only achieving elasticity of the neck and making it act like a rubber band. The more the neck is like a rubber band, the more it becomes another means of losing control of the horse's body and thus control of what you are asking your horse to do.

True lateral *flexion* of the neck is when the horse moves his head to the side just enough to allow the rider to see his eye. He does not *bend* his neck and only flexes at the poll to "give" to the bit.

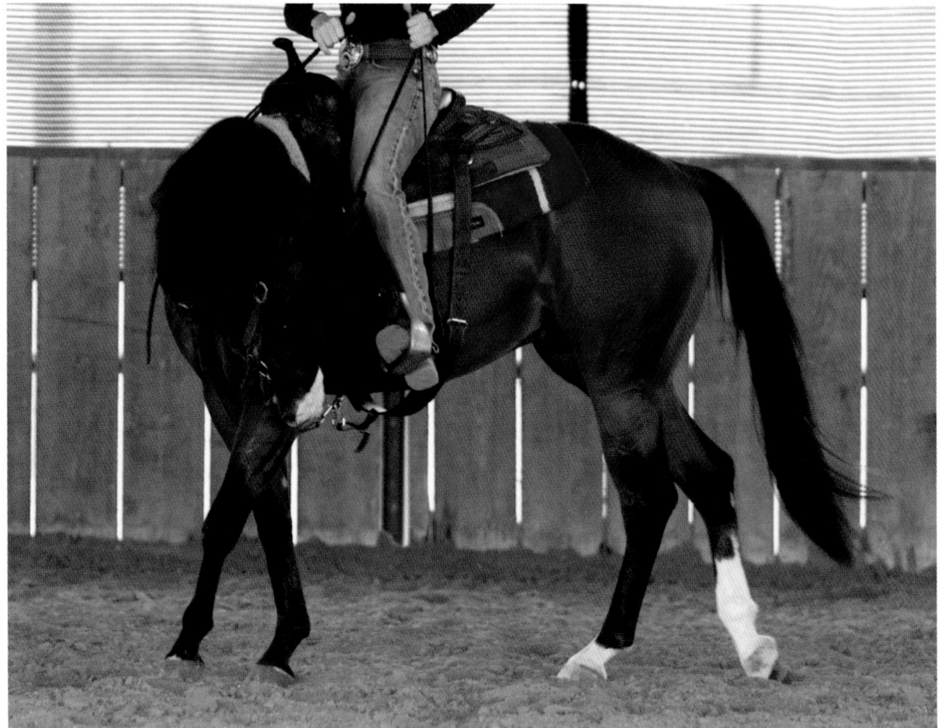

◀ *1.6* Exaggerated bending of the neck from side to side is not the way to achieve true lateral flexion and can result in false collection. Note the distressed expression on the horse's face.

Some riders incorrectly believe they are *suppling* their horse by bending his neck from side to side. However, real lateral suppleness involves the horse's *entire* body, not just his neck. Suppleness can be promoted by riding him on a curving line: The horse compacts the muscles on one side of his body while lengthening, or stretching, the muscles on the other side, from head to tail. True suppleness and lateral flexion are not done through the neck, just as true collection is not just a headset.

Artificial Gaits

An artificial gait results from the loss of correct cadence within a gait, and commonly, is seen at the trot and canter. The hind legs are "delayed" because they are not engaged with power: The trot loses its two-beat rhythm, and the canter has four beats instead of three. Artificial gaits are a sign of poor balance and a horse that is being ridden from *front to back*. Four-beating at the canter, for example, happens when a horse is too flat in his spine and has no roundness to his body. He could also be overflexed in the poll, restricted from going forward, and have more weight on his forehand. This causes his hind legs to drag behind him, which keeps him from engaging to a three-beat canter.

Collection and Longevity

Mental Health

The bottom line of training is to promote happiness and willingness from the horse. Collecting the horse naturally is putting the horse in balance through control of his body alignment. You put him in a position physically to do things the easiest way. This always results in a horse that is positive, eager, and willing. It's the ultimate in riding: the rider in control and the horse doing what you want. It is our responsibility to bring out the best in a horse. Acceptance and willingness are a must!

False collection negatively affects a horse's mental state, which is seen in his body language. Because he is physically unable to do what you are asking, he becomes frustrated and angry. Read your horse's body and he will tell you what he is feeling.

▲ *1.7* A switching tail is a sign of an unhappy horse.

▲ *1.8* A horse's ears, eyes, and mouth will also show you his discomfort or displeasure.

A horse shows his unhappiness the most through his ears and tail (fig. 1.7). He will have a sullen look and sour expression, with his ears held upright or back rather than forward. When riding you obviously can't see the tail, so you need to listen to its action. When he is switching it from side to side, pay attention to its speed. When the tail is moving quickly, something is upsetting him; when more slowly, the horse is having difficulty—either physical or mental—understanding the task at hand.

When the tail swings upward, toward, or over the back, the horse is either being "ornery" or the maneuver is really difficult for him. When he flags his tail—moving it quickly over his back much as a stallion or alpha mare does in the herd—the horse is saying, "Beware!" and taking charge. Horses that move their tail up and down, rather than side to side, are generally more difficult to work with.

Unhappiness also shows through frustration in the mouth, commonly seen as tense lips, "mouthing" of the bit, or opening of the mouth. The horse's eyes will look anxious, or when he's tired, nearly closed (fig. 1.8). His entire body will be stiff, especially through the neck. He can show roughness in his transitions, either not going forward at all or bolting ahead. Worse, his response may manifest in balking, rearing, bucking, and kicking out.

▲ *1.9* A happy horse has a pleasant, relaxed expression.

▲ *1.10* When a horse is balanced and relaxed through his body the lower part of his tail swings softly side to side.

Most horses want to behave well, but it all comes down to how we handle and relate to them. The way we choose to do these things is going to reflect in their attitude. For three decades I rode with and learned from my mentor Bobbi Steele (see sidebar, p. 5). She always told me that horses have a mind and feelings, just as we have a mind and feelings. Reflect yourself. When you get into a problem, just stop and think, "How would I feel if I were the horse?"

Physical Health

Collecting the horse isn't a "technical" style of training, it's a physical development of the horse's body. This is what takes time. Bobbi used to say, "Sure, you can run a mile. But before you get there you're going to go through stages where it doesn't feel okay, and you're going to get tired. After you practice running for a while, however, that mile becomes pretty easy."

It's the same with a horse's development: true collection will always promote his longevity, because you're developing his physique according to anatomy and biomechanics.

Rugged Lark is one of my best training examples. He retired at a young 18 years old, didn't have a "puff" in or around any joint, and had never been given a joint injection. He had been carefully brought along: built up slowly so he could be an absolute, all-around athlete that could continue to perform for a long time.

Trying to achieve collection "from the head" breaks a horse down. It places so much physical stress on him because he is not built to travel or move that way. When the horse has his poll lower than his topline and his nose behind the vertical, added strain is put on his front legs, and his back and loin muscles. His hind limb joints—hips, stifles, and hocks—are overtaxed, which is why we see so many injections being done in these areas. Muscle soreness all over the body is also something we must recognize. Read your horse through his ears, eyes, mouth, and tail (see p. 8). When in pain, he will always tell you if he resents doing what you are asking of him.

True collection promotes the soundness of any horse without obvious conformation faults, and it will show in his body language: his ears will be forward—or working back and forth and attentive; his head and neck will be (especially) relaxed; and his eyes soft; and mouth quiet (fig. 1.9). The muscles in his body will be relaxed yet defined, and the lower part of his tail will softly swing back and forth (fig. 1.10). His transitions will be smooth and he'll maintain a consistent speed in his gaits.

When you take the time to build your horse's body with training, you teach him correct self-carriage, which enables him to do anything you want to do. And, he can last forever!

William Sweeney, DVM, on Collection

For years, I have relied on Dr. William Sweeney's advice and expertise for the veterinary care of my horses. An avid nutritionist whose practice centers around show horses, Dr. Sweeney promotes physical fitness and naturally balanced trimming and shoeing of the feet as necessities for the working horse.

"I am not a trainer, but I know that a collected horse—or one that has the ability to be collected—has developed muscle tone, is stronger when he performs, and therefore has fewer physical problems for his veterinarian to deal with," says Dr. Sweeney. "Collection needs to be done in the correct stages to allow the horse to develop his muscles in a healthy way, and his mental ability at the same time. The size, breed, and age of the horse have a lot to do with how early he can begin to develop his muscle and mind. A horse who has collection will exhibit a better attitude about his job, be sounder, and all future steps in training will come easier to him."

◀ *1.11* Look at a horse's profile to evaluate his level of collection: the position of his poll; the shape of his back—uphill or downhill balance; and the forward swing of his hind legs under his body.

Recognizing Collection in Various Disciplines

There are two ways to look at a horse to evaluate his level of balance. The first and most obvious is to view his profile because that way you can see the outline of the whole horse (fig. 1.11). When you look at a horse's profile, always view from front to back, and then top to bottom. The poll has to be level with, or above the topline, of the horse. This always indicates there is less weight on his front legs and more weight on his back legs. The more advanced the maneuver, the more you have to see the horse in an "uphill," balanced frame. Based on his anatomy, for any horse to collect naturally, his hind legs must be engaged and swing well forward underneath his belly. Then, he can raise his back, lift his shoulders, and transfer weight off his front legs while elevating the poll, all of which allow the hindquarters to lower.

The second view is to look at the horse straight on (fig. 1.12). A horse must be *straight* in order to achieve the ultimate in balance, and thus collection. Natural balance requires a horse to be straight in his body, whether traveling a straight path or a curving line. Put simply, this means that the hind hoofprint lands in the front hoofprint on the same side (see p. 87). Many Western Pleasure horses are ridden with their hips canted to the inside and their head to the rail. When kept in this position and in a downhill balance for a long time, they begin to bob their heads at the canter because they lack forward motion, are crooked, and laboring in their movement.

Straightness is the only way a horse can achieve correct balance and naturally collect.

Form to Function—Flexion

There is a muscle that lies underneath and behind the jaw—between the jaw and the throatlatch of the horse (fig. 1.13). This muscle stretches when a rider correctly flexes a horse's head left and right and is accomplished through bending the horse while training him on curved lines. When this muscle stretches—after at least a year of training—the horse can easily break at the poll correctly.

If you try to flex the head by pulling it in, such as happens with overflexion (see p. 6), this muscle locks behind the jaw and you create a horse that pulls on the reins with a hard, heavy mouth. You must always remember that the horse's mouth is the most sensitive part of his body. If you go to more severe bits in an attempt to get lightness or soft responses, your horse will not only resist, overreact, and be agitated, he'll end up with a dull, or even calloused mouth.

Stand next to your horse and push the bridge of his nose onto the vertical with your hand. You should be able to easily grab that muscle behind the jaw with your first finger and thumb and hold it. If you can't, then your horse certainly won't flex easily at the poll. The exercises in this book stretch this muscle naturally—like a runner stretches his hamstrings through training and repetition—without making it large and bulky. If you take the time to gradually allow this muscle to stretch, your horse will always have a beautiful and correct set to his head.

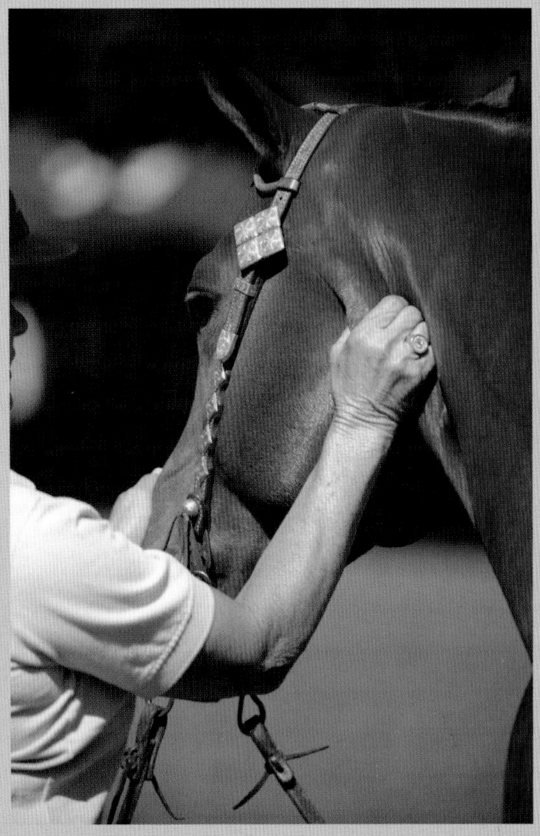

▲ *1.13* For a horse to break correctly at the poll, you must take the time to stretch the muscle behind his jaw.

◀ *1.12* A horse must be straight to achieve the balance that is needed for collection. This horse's hind feet are tracking into the same spot as his front feet.

Collection for Everyone

A rider who wants to have a fun, enjoyable ride needs a horse to steer easily, go faster or slower, be controllable in transitions, and accept his rider without any resistance (fig. 1.14). A horse that can confidently perform these common basics has learned the foundation for collection.

When a rider is balanced, she can clearly and consistently communicate with the natural aids—seat, legs, and hands. For a horse to be able to respond, he has to be balanced, too. But, he can only be balanced when the rider is balanced. The more you can control the horse's body alignment and balance through the leg and hand aids, the more he is going to accept what you are asking him to do. This formula forms a partnership where the horse and rider are working together in harmony.

◀ *1.14* Correct training builds a harmonious partnership between you and your horse.

Conformation and Collection

CONFORMATION DICTATES A HORSE'S ABILITIES. THERE ARE TWO PARTS TO conformation: conformation as it relates to physical ability—or "form to function"; and conformation as it relates to trainability (fig. 2.1). It is important to understand your horse's conformation and build your goals accordingly. For example, a long-backed horse might have a harder time changing leads in a sequence of strides or trouble jumping higher. It's not that he can't do those things, but they may be more difficult for him and take him longer to learn. A short-backed horse is usually more athletic.

There are many books with excellent illustrations showing desirable and undesirable conformation. As a child, when I started evaluating conformation in 4-H judging contests, I had to observe a horse then describe him to other attendees. This is of great value, and I recommend that when you look at a horse, you talk out loud—don't just say what you see "in your mind." If you are just beginning to learn how to evaluate a horse's build, ask your horse friends to tell you what they see when studying different horses, and ask knowledgeable professionals, such as veterinarians and trainers, to do the same. The more you hear from different people, the more *you* start to see what *they* see. It helps you shape an opinion and understanding of the way horses are built.

◀ *2.1* This Paint is built to succeed as an all-around Western horse.

▲ *2.2* An all-around Quarter Horse with enough refinement and smooth muscling to excel at Western or English events.

When analyzing conformation, stand back at least 10 feet from the horse so you can look at the complete picture (fig. 2.2). When you stand closer, your eye zeroes in on one part only, and you won't "see" his overall balance or his "angles," both of which are explained below. My general rule of thumb is if you can't see his proportions, move farther back.

The horse should be standing square or with his legs slightly offset. If the latter, the legs closest to you should be the ones further forward (front leg) and back (hind leg).

Desirable Conformation Traits

There are several desired common denominators that apply to any breed of horse. These include overall balance and correctness of the legs. (For more on balance, see p. 25, "Understanding Natural Balance.")

▲ *2.3* A hunter-type conformation that shows symmetry and balance.

Profile View

When I look at a profile, I want to see a symmetrical balance between the angle and length of the shoulder; the straightness and length of the topline from the withers to the back of the loin; and the angle and length of the hip (fig. 2.3). The angles of the shoulder and hip should match with a straight topline in between, and the shoulder, topline, and hip should be relatively equal in length.

Back

I look first for short-coupledness, which refers to the length of the back of the horse from withers to loin. A short-coupled horse is agile and athletic. I also want to see width over the loin. This gives the horse more strength to use his hindquarters.

Shoulder

The shoulder should be as close to a 45-degree angle as possible, with the withers set behind the front leg over the heart girth. This gives the horse the most freedom of movement through his shoulders and longest length of stride with his front legs.

Hip

The angle of the hip is even more important because the hindquarters are the horse's "engine." When I see a hip with a 45-degree angle and a lot of length, it tells me that horse has plenty of strength and power.

Neck

Next I look at how the neck joins, or "ties-in" to the shoulder. I want the top of the neck to be level with, or above the withers. The bottom of the neck should join the top of the chest. The length of the neck should be in proportion to the length of the body, although I don't think I've ever seen a neck that was too long.

The throatlatch area should be refined. This matters because it will make the horse more able to "set" his head in the future.

▲ *2.4 A & B* The shoulder, pastern, and hoof should all be the same angle to the ground—as shown here—and not too straight or too sloped (A). The hind leg should show correct angles from stifle to hock (B).

Front and Hind Legs

I also look at the angle of the legs. In the *front leg*, I like to see a straight line from the top of the leg, starting at the level of the elbow, through the knee and down to the pastern (fig. 2.4 A). The pastern should have the same angle as the shoulder, and the hoof should have the same angle as the pastern. In the *hind leg*, ideally you should be able to draw a straight line from the point of the buttock to the point of the hock, to the back of the fetlock joint, and then to the ground (fig. 2.4 B). This creates correct angles from stifle to hock to fetlock and is the strongest hind leg conformation.

Front and Rear Views

After I have evaluated his profile, I look at the horse from the front and the rear. From these positions I'm mostly looking at how the legs tie into the chest and the hips, and the straightness of the legs down to the hooves.

The most desirable *front leg* conformation allows you to draw a straight line from the top of the leg where it comes out of the chest, down to the middle of the hoof.

Looking at the *hind legs* from behind, you want to see a straight line from the point of the buttock through the middle of the point of the hock, down the back of the cannon bone, to the fetlock and hoof. The legs shouldn't be wider or narrower from the hips to the ground.

Breed Considerations

When you evaluate conformation, you need to know about the specific traits of various breeds and how they function. For example, Arabians excel at many events, especially endurance riding, because they're short-coupled, with a straight croup and short hip. They don't need a lot of power from behind to excel at this sport, but instead a "skeleton" that is built to last and "go" for a long time.

Warmbloods, on the other hand, generally have a more "uphill" balance with a neck that ties-in high to the shoulder, a short-coupled body, and correct angles of the hind legs. All these allow them to collect more easily—eventually to the maximum. This is why Warmbloods have such suspension to their stride and can do advanced dressage movements, such as passage and piaffe.

Undesirable Conformation Traits

Whenever I talk about conformation and how it relates to the athleticism of the horse, I'm talking about what features are in general desirable and undesirable. However, the rules are not written in stone. I love to use the example of the great show jumper, Big Ben. He's in Canada's Sports Hall of Fame. He had some traits that many people would fault, yet he was an exceptional athlete: the horse had the mental attitude and the "heart." Remember, there is no perfect horse. Interpreting conformation always comes down to weighing the pros and cons. Traits become undesirable when they deviate from the optimal, as I described on p. 19.

▲ *2.5* A long back and a neck that ties in too low are considered undesirable conformation traits.

Shoulders and Hips

As mentioned, the ideal shoulder and hip should have a lot of length, with a 45-degree angle. When the *shoulder* becomes shorter with a steeper angle, the horse is restricted by it, which interferes with his ability to reach his maximum length of stride. *A* shorter and steeper *hip* reduces the power coming from the hindquarters.

Neck, Back, and Loins

A horse that is *ewe-necked*, with a neck that ties-in below the withers or on the lower part of the chest, will have difficulty with balance and correct collection. *Long backs, narrow loins, short necks*, and *thick throatlatches* all fall into the undesirable category for a balanced conformation as they make it harder for the horse to easily collect and perform advanced maneuvers (fig. 2.5).

Front Legs

When I see a horse that is *over-at-the-knee*, I don't like it, but it is not as bad as a horse that is *calf-kneed*. I avoid the latter, because he will have trouble staying sound with hard work. When a horse is a little *offset in the knees*, meaning the cannon bones are not set perfectly in the middle of the knee, or when the horse *toes-out* or *toes-in* slightly, I'm not that concerned as long as I have a farrier who trims and shoes horses according to their conformation.

When a horse is *base-narrow* in front, meaning the front legs are wider at the chest than at the ground, I'm not worried, but when *base-wide*, it is a sign of a less-athletic animal.

▲ *2.6* Avoid a post-legged horse—one that is straight from the stifle through the hock. In addition, this horse's pastern angle is too straight, which means he will always be difficult to collect.

Hind Legs

I try to avoid *post-legged* horses where the angle from the stifle to the hock is too straight (fig. 2.6). The opposite problem is *camped-out*, meaning the hind legs have too much angle from stifle to hock. Both of these defects are signs of weakness—the horses will lack strength or soundness to perform maneuvers. They might be able to walk, trot, and canter their whole life without any difficulty, but they will be challenged to perform at higher levels. When a horse *toes-out slightly behind* it doesn't bother me. It's kind of like us: We walk with our toes slightly out because that's where we can bear our weight the easiest. However, when a horse *toes-in behind*, it puts stress on the hind leg joints.

Traits for Trainability

Through the years, I have learned there are some positive signs that a horse will be trainable. I am primarily attracted to the conformation of the horse's head. When there are traits there I feel are undesirable, I really don't look any further. I want a horse that is easy to work with, and this is related to his personality and attitude about himself and life (fig. 2.7).

Eye—This is the first part I look at. A large, dark eye means kindness and consistency. The smaller the eye, the less the horse can see so the more inconsistent he can be. A "bug eye," where you can see the sclera around the eye, generally means a horse is insecure and more difficult to work with. I've always found horses with white around the eye to be hard to bond with and slow to trust.

▲ *2.7* Rugged Lark, the most beautiful "boyfriend" I ever had! He exhibited a perfect large, dark, kind eye; a wide, flat forehead; sharp, well-set ears; large nostrils; and a small mouth with thin lips. His head is perfectly proportioned—and beautiful!

Forehead—I look for a large, flat forehead with a lot of width between the eyes. This always indicates an intelligent and very trainable horse. A horse with a smaller forehead, less width between the eyes, or a bulge or roundness to the forehead, is not as intelligent and can be more temperamental; he can be difficult at times, whether he fights you or just doesn't want to work.

Ears—An ear that is well set on the head, with width across the poll, and is of a pretty shape, always indicates a trainable horse and one that will have a beautiful expression. Arabians are the perfect example, because their ears have a beautiful shape. The type I try to avoid the most is the pin-eared horse where the ear is set on top of the head, close to the poll, and has a very upright position. A horse that can turn the face of the ear all the way around backward can be more temperamental, and one with low-set ears, commonly called "flop-eared," could lack intelligence and certainly lacks expression.

Mouth—A *short* mouth with thin lips is sensitive and responsive, which is another important aspect when it comes to trainability. Though sensitive, spirited horses require advanced riders, are not forgiving to beginning riders, and take longer to train, they can give you lightness and communication. A *long* mouth with thicker lips indicates the horse will be duller or heavier in the mouth.

Skin and Hair—Another trait that relates to sensitivity is the skin. Thin-skinned horses are always more sensitive. The way you can tell is by their hair: fine hair equals thin-skinned and coarser hair means a thicker-skinned horse that is generally more docile. Thicker-skinned horses are either easygoing and trainable, or the exact opposite—lazy with a stubborn attitude.

Nostrils—Lastly, I look at the horse's nostrils. Large nostrils with thin skin give a horse more air capacity. These belong to the horse you want to choose for demanding disciplines—endurance, reining, racing, eventing, show jumping, anything that deals with speed and distance. A horse with smaller, thicker-skinned nostrils has less oxygen available to him, and is better used for pleasure riding.

Understanding Natural Balance

A horse's natural balance starts with his conformation as assessed from a profile view (see p. 19). His balance can be classified as *uphill*, *level*, or *downhill*.(fig. 2.8).

An *uphill* balance is when the withers are higher than the top of the croup. The head and neck tie-in high to the shoulder, with the poll the highest part of the whole topline. A horse with uphill balance can distribute more of his weight on the hind legs, giving him lightness and freedom with the front legs. Breeds commonly built with an uphill balance are Warmbloods, Morgans, Arabians, and Saddlebreds. Breeds whose topline is generally *level* from withers to croup, with a neck that ties-in near the middle of their chest are: Thoroughbreds, Appendix Quarter Horses, and draft types.

▲ *2.8* This sport horse, a Quarter Horse-Holsteiner cross, shows desirable uphill balance.

A *downhill* balance is seen in a horse with a croup higher than his withers; very small withers; "mutton-withers"; or a neck that ties-in low to the shoulder. But don't be deceived when looking at a young horse. It is common for an immature horse going through various stages of growth to be higher in the croup than the withers. Horses that are built level to downhill are the stock horse breeds: Quarter Horses, Paints, and Appaloosas are probably the hardest to collect because of this conformation. With a downhill build, a horse will always struggle to transfer weight from his front legs to the back.

Natural balance plays a major role in longevity. Anatomy and mechanics dictate that a downhill balanced horse already has more weight on his front legs

▲ *2.9* Natural uphill balance and natural carriage at the walk.

and when asked to perform, he puts even more stress on them. As you know, the horse is not a "front-end" operated animal—the motor is in the back! So when you're going to stick to easier riding disciplines, the *downhill-built* horse may stay sound and last forever. But the *uphill-built* horse, whose power and energy come from behind, is the one that can be more easily trained to perform disciplines with a higher degree of difficulty involving collection, and can stay sound while doing so. Furthermore, teaching the downhill-built horse to collect to the best of his ability can help ease the stress his front end absorbs and add to his working life.

▲ *2.10 A & B* An effortless natural carriage at the trot for a hunter (A), and a natural Western jog showing uphill balance (B).

Assessing Natural Balance and Carriage

To evaluate a horse's natural balance and carriage, I like to watch him move at liberty with no attachments (fig. 2.9). A word of warning: Don't try to assess a horse's natural carriage when he's running, bucking, and playing. This is when you can see his athleticism, agility, and coordination. Wait for him to settle down—your first indication that the horse's muscles are relaxed is when the head and neck come down.

B

I like to start at the trot, a two-beat gait with diagonal leg movement that is more symmetrical than the four-beat walk or the three-beat canter (figs. 2.10 A & B). I use an oval arena to work at liberty rather than a round one so I can see the horse on a curve *and* on a straight line. Ideally, there are few distractions outside the arena so the horse isn't trying to look over the fence or wall to the outside. He needs to have a fairly straight body alignment for you to be able to accurately judge his natural carriage.

The balance you saw in your horse's conformation profile (see p. 19) is the same balance you should see in his natural carriage (fig. 2.11 A). The walk shows

▲ *2.11 A–C* A strong, stable natural uphill balance at the canter (A). This is perfect balance for doing flying lead changes (B). A horse in "inverted" balance (C) has his poll up and his back down. He cannot be collected in this frame.

you the most similar profile to the horse standing still because that's where he will be the most relaxed. At the trot, his poll will come higher, no matter what breed of horse you're dealing with. At the canter, the poll should even come slightly higher than at the trot, and you're still going to see the same profile of the horse's natural carriage as you see in his conformation when standing still (fig. 2.11 B).

I try to avoid a horse that carries himself in an *inverted* frame (fig. 2.11 C). The inverted horse's topline will be in a classic U-shape, where his poll and hip are higher than the shoulders, withers, and back. Be careful, though. Don't assume that all horses with a high poll are inverted.

How Natural Balance Influences Collection

A horse that has a natural uphill balance will be an *athletic* horse. When he's at play, you can see him stop hard, turn quickly with fluidity, and just canter off. Or, he'll jump up like an acrobat, twist, and kick, and you'll say, "Wow, he did that so easily!" He is an athlete (fig. 2.12). At the other end of the scale is the not-so-athletic horse that, when playing, stops with a hard jolt to the forehand, turns with his head up, and trots away.

At liberty, I also like to assess a horse's ability to do a flying lead change. A naturally athletic horse should be able to do one without any effort and without even thinking twice about it. But the horse that cross-canters (switches leads in front but not behind) when loose is already demonstrating he is not so athletic. It's not that he won't be able to change leads correctly, but it's going to take more time to teach him, and he will never do it as easily.

Collection is all about developing the horse's natural carriage. A horse that naturally uses the power from his hind end with less weight on his front legs is always exquisitely athletic and will always be easier to collect than the non-athletic horse.

Most riders don't take the time to develop their horse's natural carriage before training him to be collected under saddle. It can be done with the horse at liberty and by longeing him. I discuss these at length in chapter 3 (see p. 35). Or, it can be done under saddle. It's simply putting miles on a horse to allow him to learn to carry a rider, get coordinated, and acquire physical fitness.

I do a lot of riding outside the arena and hill work using my natural aids—seat, legs, and hands—to guide and control the horse's body alignment to help him to become balanced. When this happens, his speed becomes steady and he relaxes his head and neck, letting them come down to their natural position. He must become balanced like this at all three gaits before starting any training for collection.

▲ *2.12* A horse with a natural uphill balance has the potential to be very athletic—at work and at play.

Ground Training

GROUND TRAINING—WHETHER WORKING IN HAND, AT LIBERTY, LONGEING, LONG-lining, ground-driving, or longeing-and-bitting—is where you begin to build a relationship with your horse (fig. 3.1).

When you're on the ground, you can easily assess your horse's response to your commands, in addition to how much training he has had and his capacity to learn. These tell you about his personality, his ability to concentrate, and his temperament. For example, there are two types of horses—sensitive or lazy. From the ground, you can see how little it takes for the sensitive horse to react to your commands. Later, this knowledge enables you to use your aids correctly under saddle to obtain that same understanding and response. The rapport you can build on the ground is the same rapport you want to achieve under saddle.

From the ground you can observe the horse's balance; the development of his body; the coordination and strength of his movements; his action in transitions; and how long he can carry himself in a correct balance at certain gaits or speeds, as well as on circles and straight lines. Because you can only see the head and neck from on top of the horse, if you want to get this same assessment while riding, you need to be filmed on video. You have to take those images that you can see with your eyes from the ground and try to put that into feeling the results that you get from your horse under saddle.

◀ *3.1* Ground training, including longeing, is necessary to prepare for collection under saddle.

▲ *3.2* Conventional nylon halters can be easily adjusted to the horse's head. This halter has been correctly fitted for training. The noseband and side ring are no further than an inch below the horse's cheekbone.

For any horse, but especially the young horse, ground training is beneficial because he doesn't have to carry the weight of the rider. There is less impact on bones, tendons, and ligaments. It is also a great way to add variety to your training program. Yes, a horse learns through repetition. But the more you can be creative with different training techniques, the more he will like it. A well-rounded program reduces mental stress and keeps him enjoying his education.

Ground training also gives you something to fall back on when you have trouble while riding. If a horse is disobedient and wants to buck, rear, spook, or spin when I'm in the saddle, I'm not going to fight him as this jeopardizes my own safety. Instead, I'm going to regain control from the ground, correct the disobedience, gain respect, and only then continue with my training under saddle.

When your horse isn't doing what you want, he's usually asking you to stand back, assess what's going on, and improve what you're doing. Horses are smart animals and they know what you are thinking. They can't reason, but they never forget. Many people blame the horse for whatever is going wrong. I never blame the horse. Always assess and work to improve your actions to gain understanding, and you'll obtain a willing and correct response from your horse.

Ground Training Equipment

Using proper tack and equipment helps to clearly convey your commands to your horse.

Halters

I like conventional, nylon halters. I've never really worked with a rope halter because I like to have rings on the side (fig. 3.2). By using these side rings, you can control the direction of the head more precisely. Should you want to use the lead or longe line under the chin or over the nose, a rope halter does not allow you these options.

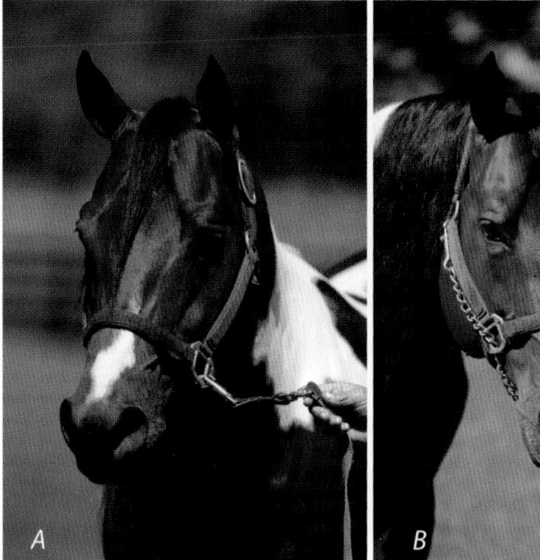

▲ *3.3 A–D* When your horse is very responsive, snapping a lead or longe line to the side ring of the halter may be all you need for perfect control (A). A flat cotton longe line is easy to manage and safe to hold. Add a chain over or under the nose with a horse that pulls or is unruly (B). When a horse responds with too much sensitivity to a longe line with a chain, an over-the-nose, snap-only attachment may smooth out his reaction (C). An under-the-nose attachment is great for the horse that carries his head too low, or for when you are longeing on grass and the horse tries to graze, thus losing his focus (D).

Lead and Longe Lines

To lead a horse, I like a lead with a snap. With any kind of training, though, I don't use a lead line—I use a flat cotton longe line (fig. 3.3 A). Cotton isn't slippery like nylon, and a flat longe line is easier to hold in my hand than a round or rolled line. I want to hold everything in my hands so there's no equipment on the ground that can get tangled around my legs.

You can also use a lead or longe line with a chain. Many people think a chain is a harsh piece of equipment, but it's truly not. Just like the bit, it depends on whose hands it's in. Yes, it can be severe when someone abuses it by jerking on the horse for every correction, but used correctly—with a little restraint—it can get more response and respect from a nonresponsive horse. My goal is always to have a horse working in-hand on a loose line. I don't want to have to pull or tug at all. A chain can help me accomplish that easily and in a short period of time (figs. 3.3 B–D).

Surcingle and Side Reins

A surcingle usually has three rings on each side for attaching side reins that can be used to create a different head position and balance (fig. 3.4). I personally like leather surcingles, although there are some nice nylon ones that aren't too

▲ *3.4* A leather surcingle with leather and elastic side reins. Note the fit of the halter over the bridle: It is high enough so that it does not interfere with the bit or the side reins. Control of the longe line is from the halter, not the bit.

lightweight or flimsy. I use a square pad under the surcingle, although if your horse's topline is in good condition without high withers or a protruding spine, and he is not overly sensitive, you can use a surcingle without a pad. It is possible to use a saddle and attach the side reins to the girth, but a surcingle gives you more options and allows you to be more consistent. Side reins are made of elastic, with a leather end that connects to the surcingle, and double elastic and a snap on the end that connects to the bit.

Whips

There are two types of whips I like for training from the ground. One is an *in-hand whip*, which is used for leading, turning, stopping, backing up, and lateral work. The in-hand whip is about 3½ feet long and has a short tassel and popper—*not* a long tassel like on a longe whip. The *longe whip* is an essential tool for training at liberty and longeing. I prefer one that's 6 feet long, not including the tassel. When a whip is too long, it's too heavy and awkward to use.

Ground Training for Collection

With all ground training, control of the horse and his response to your commands are essential and should be constantly assessed. The tools you use to get the desired response immediately are:

- Your position
- The longe line
- The whip
- Your voice

For a horse to be able physically to respond without effort, he has to be straight and balanced. He needs to focus on only you and respect what you're asking him to do. Ground training is your first opportunity to learn about straightness and balance as it relates to your horse's body position.

In-Hand Training

My goals when working in hand are: 1) no pulling on the lead; and 2) standing as far away from the horse as you can. I learned from Carol Harris (see sidebar, p. 42) that if you can accomplish these two things, you will get the very best manners and obedience from your horse.

Leading

You should be able to lead a horse at the walk and trot, stop, back up, and turn right and left without pulling on the lead. In order to do this, your shoulders must be adjacent to your horse's throatlatch or the middle of his neck. Walk parallel to the horse, with a minimum of 3 feet between you. Your in-hand whip cues the horse to go forward (see "In-Hand Whip Position," p. 40). If you want him to slow down or stop, block him in front with your hand and "lead" without pulling on the lead rope. You get results by pulling, but you can get especially keen and responsive results when you're not underneath the horse's head and constantly tugging on him.

To turn to the right while leading on the left (near) side, most people steer by pulling the lead underneath the horse's head. Instead, use the horse's instinct to move *away* from pressure to help him turn. Apply light pressure with your fist to the side of his head, where his cheekbone is, and you'll move his head to the right. Add forward motion with your voice or your in-hand whip. Walk bigger steps as you are on the outside of your horse (and the turn). He'll turn easily to the right without you having to pull on the lead.

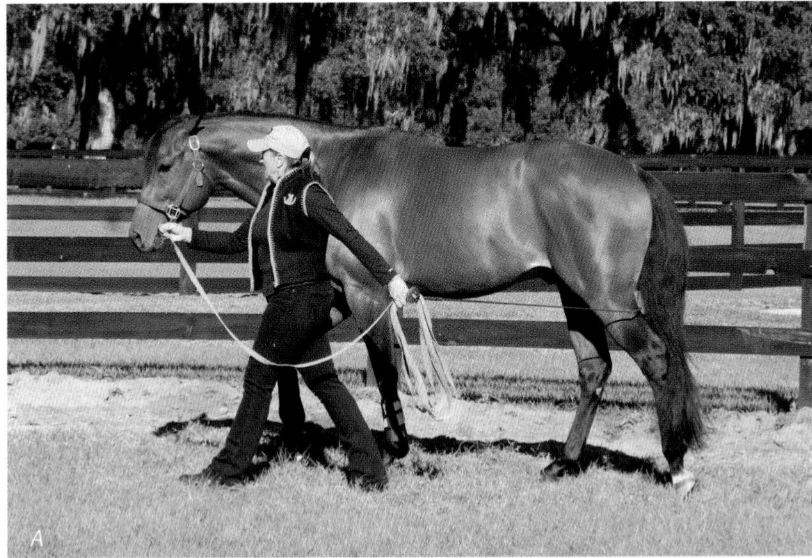

▲ *3.5 A & B* When leading your horse, use your in-hand whip to help your "go forward" aid. Note that in A my arm is straight so the whip's tassel goes behind the horse's hip. This is the correct whip position to work with the horse's natural instinct to "move away." He is "looking" at the end of the whip with his eye and ear and starting to go forward without my having to touch him. In B you see the wrong way to use an in-hand whip: My left arm is bent. As a result, the whip end goes under the horse's belly and is not in the right place to tell him to go forward. It is only encouraging resistance: The horse is moving to the right, showing displeasure with his eyes, ears, and tail.

When you want to go back to the left, shorten your step as your horse is now on the outside of the turn, use your in-hand whip, and add a light contact with the lead to direct his head to the left.

In-Hand Whip Position

Practice how to use the in-hand whip. When holding the lead in their right hand, many people keep their left arm bent as they reach behind their back to use the whip, and wind up hitting the horse in the belly or the flank. I always extend my arm straight behind my body, and then raise the whip (figs. 3.5 A & B). I let my horse see the whip, which could be all you need for the *go-forward* cue. If I need more, I touch the horse on the back side of the hip, which is where I want to activate my go-forward cue. Then, if I need still more, I lightly tap the horse to move away and go forward. Bringing my arm straight behind my body allows me to reach my horse's hindquarters.

Backing Up

To back up, I turn and face my horse and use the verbal command, "Back." Place your fist on your horse just in front of the point of the shoulder and add some pressure while keeping the horse's body straight by controlling his head (fig. 3.6). He'll move away from pressure on the shoulder and you won't have to pull on the lead. If he doesn't back up, it's because his body is not in straight alignment from poll to dock. Because you are now facing the horse, backing up is the first stage in recognizing your horse's body alignment and how it influences his response.

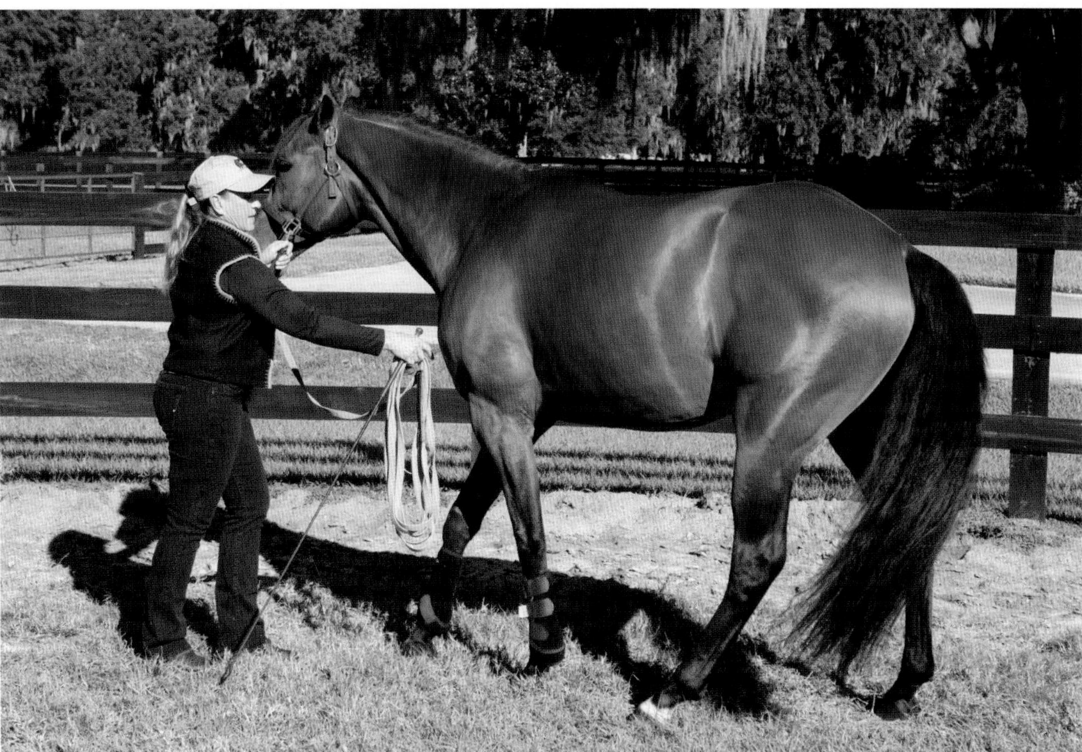

▲ *3.6* To back up your horse, position yourself next to his head with your left hand on the halter to keep him straight. Your right fist—holding the longe line and whip—contacts the point of the shoulder to initiate the backup. Here, the horse is backing easily with even steps. Note that I am watching his topline. Everyone wants to watch the legs but you cannot judge straightness this way.

At Liberty or Free-Longeing

I love working a horse at liberty to exercise him; it also gives me a chance to learn his behaviors and build a relationship with him. When he is free, he has more opportunity to go in each of his gaits. For example, during the winter in Michigan, all of the show horses were in stalls and worked in an indoor arena. We would always work a horse on the ground before riding him—chances were he was feeling "too good" because of the cold weather, wind, or reacting to the ice and

Carol Harris on Ground Training

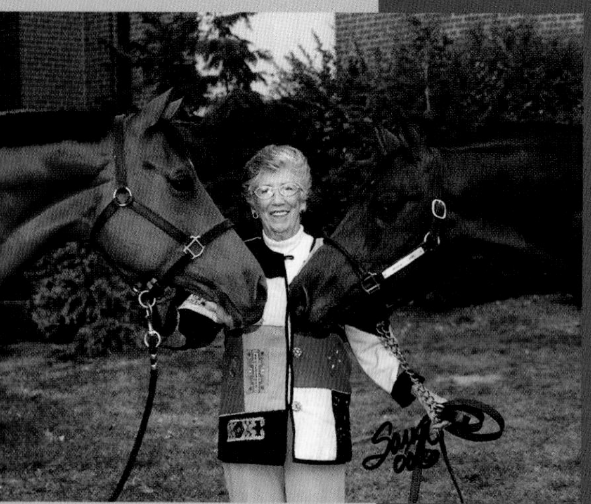

▲ *3.7* Carol proudly holds her legendary World Champion stallion, Rugged Lark (on the right) and his World Champion daughter, Jolena Lark (on the left). Notice that both Lark and Jolena are trusted to behave themselves in unusually close proximity.

Carol Harris is a lifelong horsewoman who, 60 years ago, chose to enjoy a complete career in horses and dogs. Her educated judgment, enhanced by an artist's eye and many personal philosophies, brought her unparalleled success in the demanding world of show animals. Carol, now 87, still owns and manages Bo-Bett Farm, located in Reddick, Florida, where for over 46 years she has produced many top halter and performance horses, and racehorses. Today, Bo-Bett Farm is the home of approximately 25 broodmares that primarily promote the bloodlines of her Two-Time Super Horse and Super Horse Sire, Rugged Lark.

Carol says, "I have always believed in a routine of early ground training with my horses and have witnessed the results and the bond it can create between horse and human. I have watched some men and women start horses and have observed the creation of trust that can be achieved through patience plus the development of understanding each other.

"Horse training to me can be compared to the training of dogs, kids, or 'whatever.' It should be a simple process of gaining respect and then permitting a beautiful expression from the horse to develop because of his desire to please. This process can be extremely time-consuming. It represents tedious work involving much repetition with timely rewards, however, it is way more gratifying than anything I have ever achieved in my trade.

"I do not have very many friends who have shown a desire to develop their own skills for this type of relationship with their horses, and it is frustrating to even try to explain the unbelievably positive experience that this manner of bonding brings. If we practiced more bonding and less intimidation, there would be very little need for the continual expensive vet treatments most horse owners are being forced to experience today. Also, there would be little need for the use of so many bits and gimmicks for training.

"Is it possible that we hear too many trainers tell the world how much they love their horses and yet we seldom see them show it? No one appreciates the joy of training a willing horse more than Lynn Palm. She and I have often discussed this subject and agree that the benefits of handling young horses, if done correctly, are very helpful."

snow falling from the roof. Loose in the arena, he had more opportunity to run and buck and get it out of his system in a shorter period of time. If I had tried to get the same result from longeing, it would have taken longer, with the horse more likely to pull on the longe line when he was really fresh.

Working at liberty, I prefer an oval arena rather than a round pen. In the round pen, a horse never gets an opportunity to go straight. He needs to go on straight lines as well as curves for balance. To properly work a horse at liberty, you work the centerline of the ring while your horse stays to the outside, or on the rail (fig. 3.8 A). Don't follow or chase your horse around. The goal is for your horse to move more miles than you do.

You can gain total control from your position on the ground, your voice, and your whip (fig. 3.8 B). When working at liberty or longeing, you have to be in the right place at the right time. Start by positioning yourself in the middle of your horse's body, facing his barrel (fig. 3.8 C). You can easily move to the front or back of the horse, depending on what you are trying to accomplish.

When you are facing the *middle* of your horse and working the centerline, your horse will more than likely continue in the same direction at a consistent speed. When you move toward the *front* of your horse, he's going to slow down (fig. 3.8 D). When you want to slow him down even more—or stop him and change direction—move even further to his front. When you want more forward motion, move toward his rear. Remember your goal is to move very little because your horse is working for you. You should not be getting the workout.

It takes a lot of practice to learn how to properly work a horse at liberty or on a longe line. There is a real art to moving when the horse moves and being able to coordinate your footfalls in order to stay in a parallel position to him for optimal control.

Using Your Voice

For verbal commands, I use "Walk," "Trot," "Canter," "Whoa," and "Back." When I want a horse to increase his speed, I use "Walk on," "Trot on," and "Canter on." Your whip is an aid to your go-forward cues, and your voice and your whip always work together.

Horses don't understand words exactly, but they understand tones and can learn to recognize a word. A *deep* tone is a command. If I want to ask my horse to walk, I say, "W-a-l-k" ending in a deep tone, *not* "Walk?" ending in a higher tone as if I am asking a question. The other voice I use is a *mellow* tone, which I use to reward, soothe, or instill confidence.

The length of the word is also important. Usually a sensitive horse loves it when you draw out a sound, making it longer and less abrupt: This type of horse

▲ *3.8 A–D* While working at liberty, stay parallel to your horse on the centerline (A). Here I am on the curved short side of the oval ring (B). I am positioned in the middle of the horse, keeping control of him and encouraging a forward working trot with the whip. My horse is balanced, and I send him forward by positioning myself at his hip and raising the whip, along with using my voice (C). The horse's attention is on me, as seen by his left ear and eye. I move my position to send him onto the straight line after the curve (D). Note my whip is telling the horse to stay forward in this position. Otherwise, he could slow down or roll back and change direction.

can take a longer time to process a command. With a laid-back horse, you will get quicker results when you use a shorter and more assertive sound.

Another verbal command is *clucking*, which I use to enhance forward motion or improve concentration. Some people like to use a kissing sound, which can be louder and more abrupt, but I prefer clucking because I can make the cluck soft, strong, and change the tempo more consistently.

Balance

The goal of liberty work is to control your horse's balance and natural carriage. When a horse loses it and *falls in* on the curving line, he goes faster. His body leans

▲ *3.9* The horse is falling in and "running." I position myself in the corner of the turn to move him closer to the fence, which will improve his balance. The next time around I'll start to improve his balance earlier before he gets to the area where he wants to fall in.

inward and his head position goes to the outside. When a horse loses his balance and *falls out*, his body swings outward and his head comes too far inside. Horses have more of a tendency to fall out when there is a longe line to "lean" against. They rarely do so when at liberty.

A horse generally falls in when he is running, bucking, and playing. To control this, send your horse outward on the curving line (fig. 3.9). Moving your position toward the area where he falls in, use a deep voice to tell him to "Get out," and use your whip to indicate he should "move away." As you walk toward him, your body position should be toward his front end to move him outward. The more you can keep him from falling in: 1) the more he's going to stay the same speed; 2) the more he's been exercised and suppled; and 3) the more his natural carriage and balance has been strengthened.

Your Longe Whip

1) For safety, you should always hold onto the handle of the whip. The end of the whip, or tip, should point downward. Some people carry a whip with the tip up in the air, but this can startle the horse. When you aren't using it, you always want the tip touching the ground behind or beside you. When the tip is dragging the ground, it's a useful check to remind me I'm not using the whip as a crutch to "go forward."

2) The first thing some people want to do with a longe whip is "whack" their horse on the hip to make him go forward. There are several smaller increments in which it can be used as a much more refined and lighter cue, along with your voice, to keep the horse forward. The first step is to raise the whip: When you raise the tip the horse sees it, and the higher it goes, the more he does. Second, swing the whip's tassel toward the horse's hip. If you need more of a response, snap your whip: Keeping the whip level, use a quick forward-and-back action of your wrist to flick the tassel (or "popper") out. The tassel will make a noise that gets the horse's attention and reinforces the go forward cue.

3) Never use your longe whip in an up-and-down motion. You could get some reaction from using your whip like this; however, sooner or later, your horse will become desensitized to it because you're not using the whip from behind him and working with his instinct to move away and forward. Always swing the tassel of the whip toward the back of the horse's hindquarters, or behind the horse in a sideways motion. It's best to keep the whip on a level keel because you've got more control of where the tassel is going.

4) There are times when you may want to "sting" the horse with the whip: for example, when he is ignoring you or being unresponsive to your commands. Just remember, this is always the *last step* after trying the other options above.

The hardest thing to do when you're in a paddock or any area where the horse can put his head over the fence is to keep his head straight and looking slightly in the direction of his turns with his inside ear on you. Get your horse to concentrate on you by doing lots of transitions. Change *gait* often. Change *direction* often. If these don't work, make contact with the whip on his hip. This will put his focus on you, so he respects you and pays attention to what you're doing.

There are two different ways that I like to reverse a horse. The easiest way is to turn him toward the fence. Facing the front end of your horse, walk toward him: He will turn away from you to the outside to change direction. The other way I like to reverse is to the inside. I stop the horse, ask him to come toward me a few steps, and then send him off in the new direction. With a helper you can change the horse's direction across the diagonal, which is very beneficial for teaching flying lead changes (see p. 163).

I always have my horse come to me at the end of a session. I stop the horse parallel to me, and ask him to come to me with the soft, mellow voice command "Come here." When his head is looking at me, I start backing away and he follows me. I do this because I'm nearly always asking the horse to move away, and I don't want him to fear me. When he comes to me, he's telling me he trusts me.

Longeing

Longeing can be used for exercise, conditioning, and improving the horse's natural carriage, balance, and coordination. It helps a horse's lateral suppleness and the longitudinal suppleness of the topline; it improves the flexibility of the joints through transition work; and it teaches the horse to respond to your commands while building verbal communication.

As with training under saddle, the goal of longeing is to have the horse respond to the least amount of voice and action of the whip. There's an art to longeing. It takes coordination, patience, and time to do it well. Remember, when you can get control of your horse and understand him from the ground, it will assure you of more success under saddle.

To start a horse on the longe line in a controlled fashion, I always start out from a leading position. Stay parallel to the horse, move your whip from your left hand to your right—always behind your back—and create a "triangle" position with your horse: You face the middle of your horse's barrel; your longeing arm is one side of the triangle; your horse is the second; and your whip is the third side.

When longeing to the left, for you to stay parallel to and the same distance from the horse, cross your right leg in front of your left as you walk (fig. 3.10 A). Longeing to the right, cross your left leg in front of your right. Always keep a light contact to the horse's head with your longe line.

One rule I always follow when I start is to ask the horse to walk at least one full circle on the longe line. This helps stop him from trying to take off, buck, and run—you can have controlled play thereafter (see p. 50). After that, for the most part, the session consists of walking, trotting, trot to canter, canter to trot, and trot to walk. When I have a more sensitive type of horse, or one that's more anxious, I stay with a slower gait and ask for more transitions to keep the horse's focus on me.

▲ *3.10 A & B* The longeing circle size should be large enough to allow your horse to move with coordination and in balance. Note my right leg crosses in front of my left to allow me to stay parallel to my horse (A). Toss your longe line toward your horse's head to encourage him to move outward on a larger circle (B).

I always try to create a circle size in which my horse is coordinated and balanced. When his legs move quickly, the circle could be too small. When your horse is lethargic and not going forward, your circle is too big and you're not going to have any connection. When you're walking parallel to your horse, and you want him to make a larger circle or move away from you, toss the longe line toward his head (fig. 3.10 B). Use the horse's instinct to move away from it.

Similar to liberty work, the goal of longeing is to improve and control your horse's balance by controlling his body position (see p. 43). When a horse *falls in on a circle*, his head looks to the outside, and most people's natural instinct is to pull the head in with the longe line (fig. 3.11 A). Don't do it! Pulling on the head only brings the head in for an instant, and that doesn't fix the falling in. You must toss the line toward him to make him go on a wider, curving line. Then, with each revolution, remember the weak spots where he falls in and work to improve them before your horse gets there.

◀ *3.11 A & B* In A is an example of a horse falling in. His head is positioned to the right on a left circle, and his weight is obviously distributed on his left legs. This is a horse in a poor balance. The second most common loss of balance is falling out, as shown in B. The head is positioned too far to the inside, which shifts his legs to the outside. You will feel your horse pull on the longe line when this happens.

When he *falls out on the circle*, encourage forward motion to improve his balance (fig. 3.11 B). Send him forward by opening your longeing arm to a wider stance, and use your voice and whip. Pay attention to your position, because his falling out can be exaggerated if you walk toward the horse rather than staying parallel. A horse's herd instinct is often the reason he will tend to fall out as he passes the gate or in the direction of the barn. When he falls out on one side of the circle, he usually falls in on the opposite side.

When you have your horse supple on a circle, without falling in or out, then move on to a straight line. To do this, move your body position slightly forward toward the horse's head and extend your stride in order to stay parallel to the horse, so you are essentially walking alongside him. You return the horse to a circle by shortening your step and moving your position back to the middle of your horse's body.

A longeing session should include: different size circles, turns to straight lines, and straight lines to turns. Here is a common pattern I use: medium circle to straight line, medium circle, smaller circle, medium circle, straight line, larger circle. A good test of the horse's balance is to longe on a smaller circle and ask him to spiral to a larger circle. If he can do so without falling in or out, you have truly exercised him correctly.

Controlled Playtime on the Longe Line

When a horse is acting up and feeling good, I work him at liberty (see p. 4). I may want him to jump and buck—especially when he's young—but I may not think I'll be able to hold onto him on a longe line. I encourage him to play while he's loose so I have a greater chance of control on the longe line later.

Sometimes, you won't have the opportunity to work at liberty first. This is where controlled playtime on the longe line comes in. Prepare yourself for controlled playtime by holding the longe line with two hands. Maintain a parallel distance, and control his head by keeping him slightly looking inward: If the head gets to the outside, the horse can use his body weight against you and get away.

Keep your circle smaller than usual. This gives the horse less opportunity to get away and also makes him work harder so he'll calm down more quickly. I generally work at the walk and trot first—the canter is where he's the most apt to play.

When he stops running and tossing his head and I start to see his legs slow down, I ask for the trot. I may ask him to go right back to the canter and clap my hands or stomp my feet and try to make him play again. I've already assessed my circle size and I'm anticipating it with two hands ready on the longe line, so I'm ready to keep playtime under control.

You learn from longeing that he'll play more going in one direction: usually on his stiffer side or the side on which he falls in more. After he's gone both ways, I'll test him again with transitions to see his level of energy. When he performs a transition immediately, especially slowing down, his playtime is over.

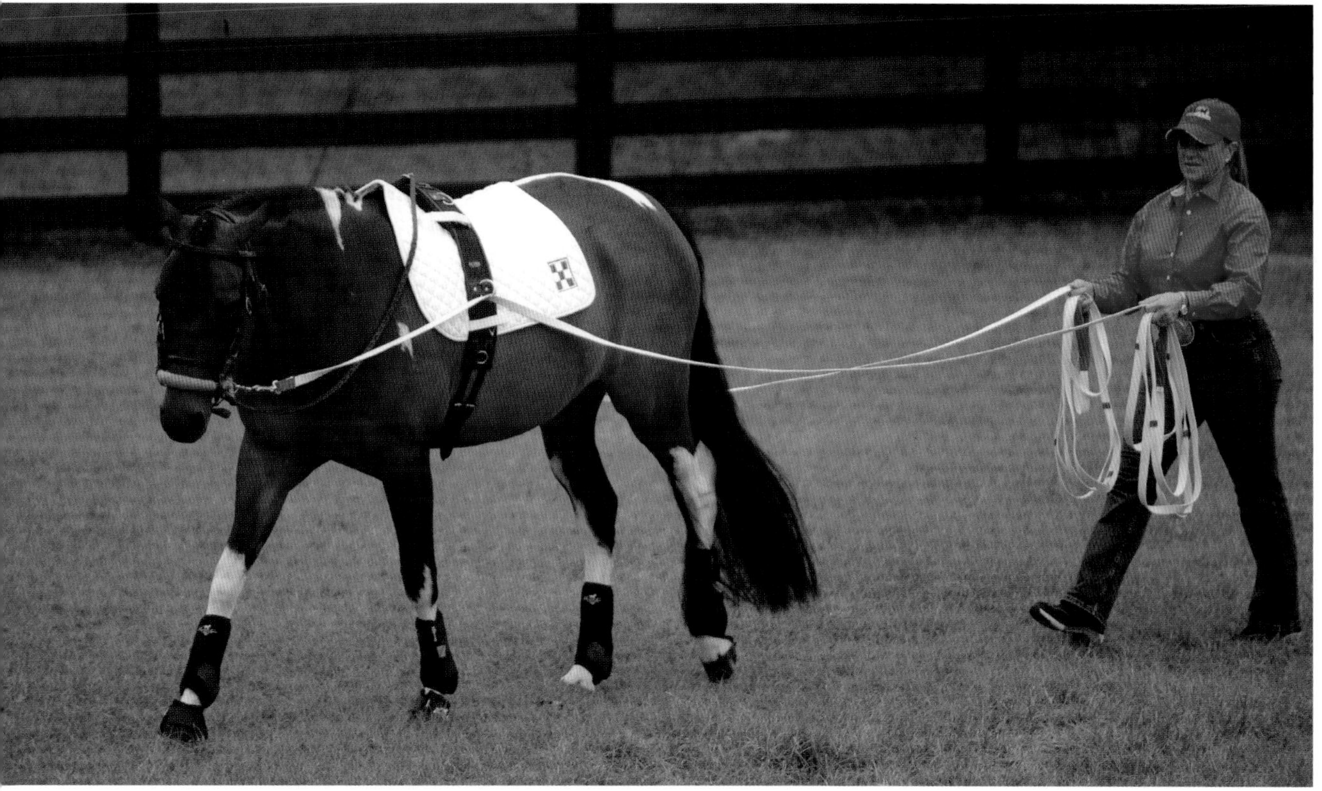

▲ *3.12* Ground driving teaches a young horse to steer and "give" to the bit, and adds variety and low-stress training to your older horse's routine.

Ground Driving

For me, ground driving a young horse is an absolute necessity (fig. 3.12). I would never get on if he did not confidently "steer" in both directions, stop, and back up. This way when you get on him and start to walk, steer, stop and back, you're not confusing him. (One of my goals is never to confuse a horse.) Older horses also benefit from ground driving because of its usefulness as a low-impact conditioning tool and low-stress training activity that adds variety to your program.

People also benefit from ground driving. I love using it to teach people to see their horse's body alignment. When you're behind the horse, you truly get to see from the poll, to the crest of the neck, the withers, the back, the top of the croup, and the dock. You get to see your horse's spinal alignment and the footfall of his hind legs tracking to the front legs. This helps you when it comes time to control your horse's body alignment while *straight* and *bending*, which I'll get into in later chapters.

Use a snaffle bridle, surcingle, and a pair of long lines or longe lines to ground drive. Before you begin, your horse must accept the feel of the lines on his side. Be sure to desensitize him. Let him drag one line, and then both behind him until he is accustomed to their feel.

To begin, attach the long lines to the bit and run them through the side rings of the surcingle. Use the long lines as if you were longeing, although you will be *behind* your horse. Walk both circles and straight lines, and change directions. Unlike the single attachment of a longe line, ground driving gives you the flexibility to do many different kinds of figures, such as serpentines and figure eights.

Ground driving teaches the horse to give to the bit by flexing his head left or right. He learns to *steer* by giving to the bit from your open rein that positions his head to initiate a turn, and learns to *yield* from your indirect rein against his barrel and/or hip as he moves away from pressure to turn. When you close your hand or fingers it means slow down, and you can use a give-and-take action with your rein aids to teach your horse not to pull.

All of this is done at the walk and trot. As the horse advances in his training, you can get him to be a little more responsive by making tighter turns and shorter straight lines, or asking him to change speed within a gait. I use the same rein aids ground driving as I do for under saddle work (see p. 80).

When my husband Cyril and I got married, he gave me my choice of honeymoon, and I wanted to go to Vienna, Austria, to see the Spanish Riding School. The master of the riders did a solo performance with a horse on long lines. He didn't use a surcingle so there were no rings to keep the long lines in order, just two lines from his hands to the horse's mouth. He walked very close to the horse's back legs with his hands nearly touching the horse's hips. I watched half-pass at the trot and canter, passage, piaffe, two-tempi and one-tempi lead changes, and canter pirouettes—all with a man on the ground behind a horse. I couldn't believe what I was seeing.

It was so special because he was doing movements usually only achieved under a rider. There is a lot you can do on the ground, much more than I can share with you in this book. I can share, however, what the majority of horses and people can do to build a foundation of training, understanding, and trust with their horse.

Longeing-and-Bitting

Longeing-and-bitting, also known as "bitting a horse up" with side reins, is a low-impact training technique to exercise the topline muscles of the horse (fig. 3.14).

Physical Fitness

▲ *3.13* Ponying is a great low-stress way to add variety to your training program, keeping your horse physically fit and happy.

Low-impact ground training is a great way to give "forced" exercise, that is, exercise that is part of a horse's daily routine. It builds a horse's physical fitness, which is absolutely necessary for collection (fig. 3.13). Many people think that when a horse is turned out all the time, he is getting exercise. However, a horse will only exert himself for a release of energy: He's not going to exercise daily to stay fit.

A wonderful vet I've learned so much from is Dr. William Sweeney from Madison, Wisconsin. He encourages building a horse's physical fitness. He compares the horse to the football player who only plays during the season and does nothing else the rest of the year. He is far more susceptible to injury, because he is not as fit as he could be if he exercised year-round. Also, the older a horse gets, the more important it becomes that he stays fit with a year-round exercise program, because like a person, it is harder for him to come back and realize the same level of fitness he had prior to any letdown time.

You have to be smart and vary your training to give your horse low-impact, low-stress workouts at times to keep him physically fit. So you can assess his fitness, I recommend you make a log of your training. Record how far you ride and your lessons, and write down your horse's overall reactions. Then, you can look back and see that last month, when you rode for a certain period of time your horse was really tired and was puffing a lot, but this month he wasn't even breathing hard. Knowing your horse's fitness level is important if you want him to perform to the best of his ability, no matter what you are asking him to do.

▲ *3.14* Longeing-and-bitting is a low-impact exercise to strengthen the topline muscles and teach the horse to start giving to the bit and breaking at the poll. A horse should be proficient at being longed in a halter alone before longeing-and-bitting.

Too many people use longeing-and-bitting just to get a "headset," which is not correct. In my training program, longeing-and-bitting is a tool to help further the training of the young horse, in particular to have him start to shape his body while moving. It allows me to continue to perfect my longeing practice, while also asking the horse to move in a specific way. The first thing a young horse learns is to accept the tension of the reins without resistance—that is, give to the bit.

By the young horse, I mean the four- or five-year-old. Longeing-and-bitting should never be done with a yearling or two-year-old. I do not even recommend it for a three-year-old unless the horse is mature enough physically and mentally, and even then, it should only be used in the most basic stages.

There are some very specific criteria you and your horse must meet prior to longeing-and-bitting (fig. 3.15). Before you use side reins, both of you need to be very proficient at longeing in a halter alone. The horse should longe easily at all three gaits and do all the transitions, upward and downward, without any problems. He should respond very well to voice commands. There are also four responses I look for under saddle before I employ longeing-and-bitting:

▲ *3.15* A horse in perfect balance at the canter. You can see the definition of the topline muscles and his uphill balance. The horse is accepting and giving to a light contact while breaking at the poll beyond the vertical.

1) "Giving" to the bit: A horse gives to the bit by flexing his head left or right through the action of an *open* rein. He feels direct pressure on the bit and gives to it.

2) "Yielding" to the bit: A horse yields to the bit through the action of an *indirect* rein, or *neck rein*. He feels the indirect pressure of the rein against his neck and yields to it.

3) Slow down: The horse should know how to slow down by giving when you pick up on the reins or close your hands on the reins.

4) "Giving" while going forward: The horse should be learning to give to the bit as he goes forward and start to gently break at the poll with his nose beyond the vertical.

Fitting and Adjusting Side Reins

As you prepare your horse for longeing-and-bitting, something too often overlooked is proper length of the side reins from the surcingle to the bit. You have to adjust the reins according to the horse's conformation. Before you ask your horse to move, look at your horse's natural head and neck carriage and fit the side reins so they are fairly loose, just establishing a contact with the horse's mouth (fig. 3.16 A). The side reins must not be tight: When they put too much pressure on the horse's mouth, he will resist by raising his head, or he'll evade by dropping his poll and moving his head behind the vertical (fig. 3.16 B). Too-tight side reins subject the horse to physical and mental stress, which is why it is important to adjust them properly from the start—and always respect this rule.

Some people attach the longe line through one side of the snaffle bit ring, over the top of the poll and connect it to the bit on the other side. I don't because I don't want the horse to feel any other tension on the mouth except for the side reins. Instead, I fit a conventional halter over the bridle, and up high enough so it doesn't interfere with the bit in any way. Then, I attach the longe line to either a side ring on the halter, or over the horse's nose. On the surcingle, the side reins should be attached to the top ring. The lowest ring, where the side rein would extend straight and parallel to the ground, is for the most advanced stages of collection only (fig. 3.16 C).

A training session should never start with longeing-and-bitting. First, always work your horse at liberty or on a longe line without being bitted—in both directions and at all three gaits. He must show that he doesn't have extra energy and want to play, and he's ready to work before you do any bitting. Then, follow the same routine you use for regular longeing when you do longeing-and-bitting, making use of circles of varying sizes as well as straight lines (see p. 47).

As your horse progresses in his training, gradually adjust the side reins so there is a slight tension in the reins, and move the side reins to a lower ring on the surcingle. For the first several months to one year, the horse will carry his head slightly ahead of the vertical at approximately a 45-degree angle. Your horse is learning to relax the head and neck down when he feels the tension of the side reins, give to the pressure of the bit, and go forward without ever going on the forehand.

As you tighten the side reins and move to lower rings on the surcingle, you are asking your horse to start shortening up his neck a little bit more, bring his nose closer to the vertical, and elevate the withers so he can raise the neck and the poll. This is asking your horse to work more in an *uphill balance* in a more collected fashion.

I cannot stress enough that this is *not* for young horses. This stage of longeing-and-bitting comes after months and years of training, when the horse has learned to

▲ *3.16 A–C* Properly adjusted side reins for the beginner horse are attached to the top ring of the surcingle, and the reins have a light contact with the bit (A). Side reins should never be adjusted too tight. Notice this horse's sour expression and his tense, locked mouth (B). As your horse's training progresses, move the side reins down the rings on the surcingle (C).

▲ *3.17* The inside rein should not be tight so as to cause the horse's neck to bend. If it does, the horse will fall out on the circle (see p. 49).

shorten up his body without ever losing forward impulsion, and to engage and use his back. That's advanced collection, and when you are at that level, you use a lot of longeing-and-bitting to warm up an older horse, to do a workout session instead of riding, or to help get a horse more comfortable at horse shows. It's a very effective tool that you can use on a regular basis.

Often, people bit up a horse with the inside side rein too tight (fig. 3.17). They think they are making the horse bend, when actually all they are doing is bending the neck: the horse moves the shoulders and hips out and loses straightness. Try to keep the exact same length of side rein on each side. When you have a horse that is very stiff on one side, maybe you can tighten the inside rein a little bit, but only enough to ask for flexion of the head, not a bending of the neck.

In no case is it acceptable or justifiable for the horse to be put in an unnatural head and neck carriage from tightness of the side reins. This is counterproductive. When people try to bring the nose to the vertical with side reins, they create a *false collection*, which is never the correct way to longe and bit a horse (see also p. 71). When the side reins are too tight, you not only teach the horse to hollow his back, but more often than not, you also teach him to go *behind the vertical*, which is a difficult problem to correct. Your horse is asked to move in a way that is physically stressful, totally unbalanced, and not productive whatsoever in terms of muscle conditioning, and stamina (fig. 3.18).

Longeing-and-bitting prepares and helps the young horse to give to the bit while going forward. While longeing-and-bitting, you must always keep in the back of your mind that sacred principle—"*from back to front*" (see p. 2). Anything that constricts the horse in front is going to make the horse want to resist with his head and neck, hollow his back, and not engage his hind end at all, which is the exact opposite of what we want to accomplish.

▲ *3.18* Longeing-and-bitting is not a quick fix and can do more harm than good if not done properly. Here, the horse is resisting contact, is behind the vertical, and falling out—all at the same time.

It's easy to see if a horse has been longed and bitted properly by looking at his neck when you are riding. When its base is wider than the poll, the horse has been worked properly. But if the area by the poll is wider than the base, it usually means the horse has been forced into an artificial headset with side reins and/or draw reins. You will also see very little muscling along the topline, a weak loin, and an ill-defined croup.

Too many people use longeing-and-bitting as a quick fix, and the horse is the one that suffers. Done properly, it can be a very useful training technique. If not used properly, you can do more damage than good. If you have never done it before, make sure you have professional guidance.

Before You Saddle Up

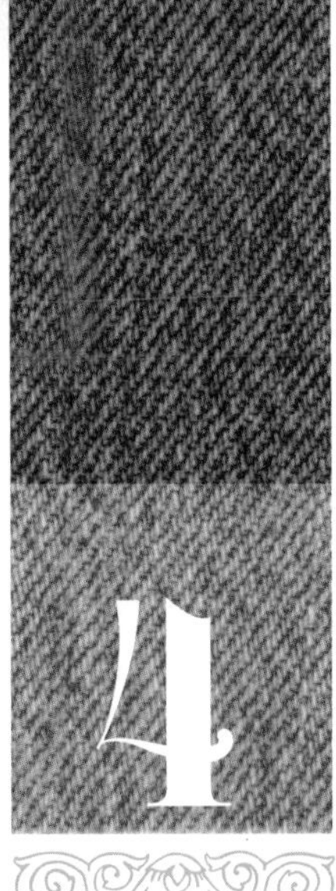

NATURAL COLLECTION IS AN ATTAINABLE GOAL FOR EVERYONE, NO MATTER WHAT breed of horse you ride or what type of saddle you choose. However, there are certain skills you should have before starting the riding exercises in this book.

There are three main topics all riders should know about:

1) Rider position and balance
2) Use of natural aids for communication
3) Rider responsibility to control the horse's balance

Rider Position

As a rider, you need to have knowledge of the correct riding position, which is how you achieve balance. This position puts the rider in the middle of the horse's center of gravity, which is behind the withers in the middle of his back. It is a *vertical* position. From a *profile view*, you should be able to draw a downward line from your ear to the middle of your shoulder, middle of your hip, back of your heel, to the ground. From the *front view*, the middle of the rider's body and chin should line up with the crest of the horse's neck, with the rider's spine in line with the horse's spine (figs. 4.1 A & B). The position may vary by discipline. For example, in

◀ *4.1 A & B* Proper riding position doesn't change with the type of saddle you use: A line should be able to be dropped vertically from the rider's ear, through the shoulder, hip, and heel, to the ground.

a two-point jumping position (profile view), the rider's position is a line from the ear to knee, toe, and the ground. This still puts the rider's weight over the horse's center of gravity.

To sit properly in a saddle, no matter what kind it is, you must sit centered and on your seat bones evenly. The easiest way to feel the correct position on your seat bones is to sit with a straight back and upper body in a hard chair (fig. 4.2 A). You should feel your seat bones, which are at the bottom of the pelvis, cushioned by your buttocks. When you tilt forward with your upper body—the most common loss of correct position for riders—you sit on your crotch with very

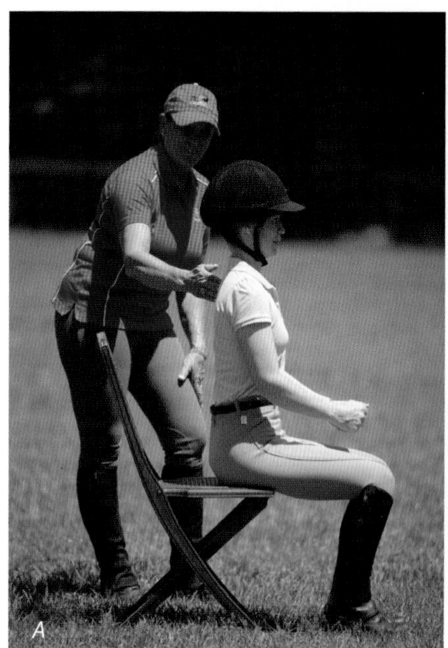

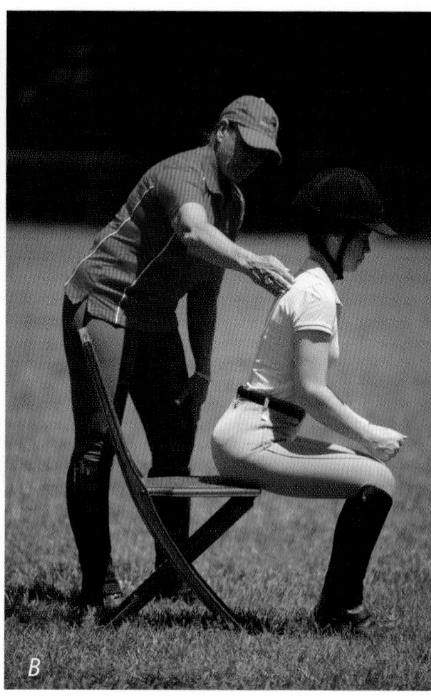

▲ *4.2 A–C* Sitting on a hard chair with a straight back is an easy way to find out what it should feel like when you sit on your seat bones correctly in the saddle (A). A rider sitting on her crotch and tilting her shoulders forward is a common sight (B). She needs her thighs, stirrups, and/or hands to stay in balance, which is incorrect. Less commonly seen is a rider pushing her shoulders too far back, which puts her out of balance onto her tailbone (C). This position is not only uncomfortable but also incorrect.

little weight in the saddle (fig. 4.2 B). This results in you bouncing. And when you lean back with your upper body, you sit on your tailbone—uncomfortable and also an incorrect position (fig. 4.2 C).

An incorrect riding position will stress the horse in some way because the horse has to adjust his legs and his movement to compensate for the rider's balance (figs. 4.3 A & B). Sooner or later the horse is going to start resenting his rider. Riding in proper position and balance is the only way that you can continue to get positive, willing, and more correct responses. When I work with riders at clinics, 95 percent of the time I can get improved responses from the horses by only working on improving the riders' positions.

Maintaining the correct position is the only way you can use your aids clearly and consistently. When you are a balanced rider, you can relax, think, and tell your body what to do with timing and coordination. You should also be able to look up and in front of your horse—a "must" for control—instead of focusing down. Riding with your eyes up and in front opens up another dimension of what riding is all about: feeling.

As riders, we are all challenged by a natural instinct to look at the horse's head and neck in order to control him. Until you can *feel* what you and your horse are doing at all times, you have to concentrate hard to break this natural instinct. When you look at the head or neck, the horse has his mind in front of yours. When you look in front of your horse, you have your mind and decisions in front of your horse's, thus gaining more control at all times!

▲ *4.3 A & B* A common rider mistake is to lean too far forward and pinch with your lower leg for balance (A). Note the horse's unhappiness because of the extra weight on his front legs. Although less common, it is just as incorrect to lean too far back (B). The rider's legs are forward and braced, and her hands are raised in an effort to maintain her balance.

▲ *4.4* Bobbi Steele taught me at a young age to communicate with my horse through my seat and legs more than my hands, allowing me to ride bridleless.

▲ *4.5* To do the collection exercises in this book, you must be comfortable at all three gaits, especially the canter.

Rider Balance

My childhood riding instructor Bobbi Steele was a wonderful influence (see p. 5). She taught me that if I wanted to participate in horses and riding, I had to learn to become a rider who is absolutely, 100 percent balanced on her horse.

As a young rider, I had to learn how to ride without my reins. Of course, it started with countless hours of lessons on the longe line before I progressed to a paddock and then an arena. She would always tell me that if I could learn to ride really well without reins—walk, trot, canter, turning, and changing direction—that she'd teach me to ride bridleless (fig. 4.4). As a kid, that was the ultimate goal.

What Bobbi was really doing was teaching me to learn to balance through my seat and ride from my waist down. This taught me to communicate through my seat and legs more than my hands. She is the reason I ride bridleless. I did a lot of it before Rugged Lark and it all came from her.

My first job out of high school was at Frontier Town, a tourist attraction in upstate New York. I was hired to perform an act with my horse where I jumped through a rotating hoop of fire without a bridle, three times a day, seven days a week, for three summer months. Wow, did this teach me a lot about keeping a horse performing willingly and correctly! The more I improved as a rider, the better the responses I was able to get from my horse.

Balance allows you to ride without interfering with your horse's performance. When a horse isn't doing what I want, I always ask myself, "Lynn, how's your balance, how's your position?" Position equals balance, and balance equals a rider who can be functional.

Rider Skills

To perform the exercises in this book, you need to be proficient in the saddle at the walk, trot, and canter, and not have any fear of the horse you are riding. (fig. 4.5) You should be able to do all simple upward and downward transitions from halt to canter, and control the horse through three speeds in all gaits, that is using his *natural* length of stride, a *lengthened* stride and a *shortened* stride.

Terminology

In the equestrian world, each discipline has its own terminology and jargon. English horses "trot" and "canter" while Western horses "jog" and "lope." To avoid confusion between working trots, extended trots, jogs, and walks, I have chosen some universal terms for this book. The three primary gaits will be referred to as "walk," "trot," and "canter." The three speeds/stride lengths within each of those gaits will be referred to as "natural," "lengthened," and "shortened." As you practice the exercises in each chapter, keep in mind that if you are riding an English horse, your trot will be different from the Western horse, and that's okay.

Horse Skills

No matter what level of training your horse has completed, he will benefit from the exercises in this book. Young horses that have not yet been started under saddle will have a lot to gain from most of the ground-training exercises in chapter 3 (see p. 35). For the riding exercises, a horse should have at least 10 to 12 months of the ground-training and under-saddle work to develop the natural carriage and physical fitness he needs to complete the exercises.

All horses should be given the time under saddle to develop their natural carriage before any real training begins. One year at Equitana, I saw champion German dressage rider Reiner Klimke give a lecture on how dressage horses are trained in Germany. I'll never forget some of the things he said. Number one, nothing is done with their horses until they are three years old. They give the horses time to grow up, physically and mentally, turned out in a natural environment.

Second, for the first year of training, they just ride their horses and let them learn how to carry themselves. I was so excited to hear that! Because that is what so many people *don't* do when they start young horses: They don't give them the time to learn to carry a rider, walk, trot, canter, go up and down hills, and gain a natural carriage according to their conformation. A horse needs to learn to carry himself on a loose rein without the rider's help. For your horse's happiness and longevity, please take the time and allow your horse to get strong and naturally balanced before training him for collection.

When you have a young or green horse just starting the groundwork, you will be able to build his physical fitness as he progresses through my exercises. But if this is your first time teaching any horse how to collect, it is desirable to have an older horse to practice on and master the exercises with before working with the young horse.

Carla Wennberg on Collection

▲ *4.6* Carla Wennberg performing a sliding stop.

AQHA Professional Horseman and Judge Carla Wennberg grew up showing horses and, as an adult, continues to make horses her life and career. Currently a coach at St. Andrews Presbyterian College in Laurinburg, North Carolina, Carla was named the Professional's Choice AQHA Professional Horsewoman of the Year in 2009.

"I have known Lynn since I was 13 years old—I am now 50!," says Carla. "I first saw her ride a dressage horse at our North Carolina State Fair show. I was so amazed and wanted to have her knowledge. I wanted to be like her, I wanted to ride like her, and I especially wanted to train like her! She was one of my first trainers and she influenced me in so many ways, but in particular, about care and respect for the horse.

"She taught me as a student to ride with 'feel' and to take time to develop the horse. I have carried this all my life as a trainer and instructor.

"The most important thing Lynn taught me about collection is to develop forward movement and natural carriage. You have to have these *first* before you can ask a horse to bring himself back with more engagement and balance. All of it takes time, and as Lynn always says, *you must take the time*!

"To have a great 'pattern' horse, whether it is for Western Horsemanship or dressage, he must be a 'collected' horse."

The Horse and Rider Team

It is an absolute must that the horse suits his rider. Too many people don't take the time to keep assessing the suitability of their horse to their skill level, goals, and personal commitments. This should be a constant evaluation as you own and train your horse.

I ask people two simple questions that should be answered with a resounding "YES!" for their horse to be a suitable mount for them. The first is, are you safe? It is impossible to be comfortable on a horse if you don't feel secure. You have to trust your horse in every way. There is no way safety can be completely guaranteed with horses, but as the rider, you must trust your horse.

The second question I ask is, are you having fun? When you can have a comfortable ride where you are in control; can extend your gait; slow down; steer easily; or anything else you ask for, you will have fun.

Tack

As you work toward collection, one of your goals should be learning to "read" whether your horse is accepting you or not. Tack becomes an essential part of this. Riding is a sport, and if you want to do a sport well, you've got to have the right equipment. Common sense dictates that when you first start riding, you're going to get more economical equipment. But when you realize you are serious about the activity, you have to invest in quality. You must also know how to fit this tack to both you and your horse.

Saddle Fitting

The basics of saddle fitting apply the same for most saddles, whether English or Western. The number one principle of saddle fitting is for you to focus on the horse. When you buy a pair of shoes that don't fit, you're going to have difficulty walking. So, a saddle that does not fit the horse, is going to keep him from performing properly.

STEP ONE

First, position the horse on a flat, level surface. Stand him square, making sure he isn't standing with a hind foot cocked. Allow him to hold his head and neck naturally, keeping his head and neck straight.

Position a saddle—without a girth or pad—properly on the horse's back, not too far forward or back (fig. 4.7). Place it just behind the horse's shoulder blade.

English saddles have a small pocket underneath the flap that marks the point of the tree, while on Western saddles, it is the bottom of the swells. You never want the point of the tree, which is usually wood, plastic, or fiberglass, to actually sit on the horse's shoulder. Imagine carrying a backpack with the strap pinching your shoulders the whole hike: It's going to keep you from wanting to walk forward. This is what happens when the tree touches the horse's shoulders—it will really pinch the horse.

▲ *4.7* To begin saddle fitting, position the saddle properly on the horse's back without a pad or girth.

▲ *4.8 A & B* A saddle tree and front panels properly fitted to the horse's shoulders. The front portions of the panels contour to the horse's body.

When a saddle is positioned too far back, it is the same as you carrying your backpack too low. Its weight pulls you backward, and it's hard to step forward. The rider's weight is located toward the horse's loin area, which by nature is not weight-bearing, and he will have difficulty lifting his back and "pushing" with his hind legs.

Once the saddle is properly positioned, stand 10 to 12 feet away and look at the horse's profile, remembering to keep him standing square on all four feet with his head and neck straight. Assess how level and balanced the saddle looks. Is it pitching forward toward the withers or backward toward the rump? When a saddle is level, most of the paneling underneath will be in even contact with the horse's back.

Next, stand 2 to 3 feet in front of your horse facing the point of his shoulder. Look directly at the front panels and see how they fit the contour of the shoulder (figs. 4.8 A & B). Get as close as you need to see if there are any gaps. Look at both sides of the horse—just because the left front panel fits well doesn't mean the right side will too.

Once you have examined the front panels, go to the pommel. Stack your fingers vertically and slide your hand between the top of the withers and the bottom of the pommel, which will give you an idea of the clearance there. An approximate correct fit is two to three fingers of space.

◀ *4.9* With any saddle, including a dressage saddle like this one, all the underpaneling needs to be in even contact with the horse's back.

Finally, look at the length of the saddle in relation to the length of the horse. As a rule, you never want the back of the saddle to be past the horse's last rib, because the rider's weight will be too far back toward the loin. This is especially important with the stock horse breeds that have a tendency to be short-coupled.

STEP TWO

Attach a girth, but still without a saddle pad. Make sure the girth is balanced, attached evenly on both sides, and the saddle is centered on the horse. Tighten the girth just enough to bring the saddle in contact with the horse, but leave it loose so you can slide your hand between the saddle and the horse. Repeat the assessments you made in Step One. With the saddle now closer to the horse's body, you can get a more accurate assessment of saddle fit.

When it comes to saddle fitting—no matter what type of saddle or discipline—the more surface that is in contact with the horse, the more comfortable it is for him because the weight of the rider is distributed over a larger area (fig. 4.9). What you want to avoid at all costs is a localized pressure point. Going back to the backpack example, this is like you having all its weight centered over one area—over your right collarbone, for instance. The pain is all you feel after a while, and you would do anything to get rid of it. It's the same for the horse.

With the girth attached, pay closer attention to the fit of the front panel in relation to the shoulder. You do not want any daylight between the front panel and the horse: The contour of the front panel should shape exactly to the bottom of the withers and the shoulder.

At this point, I use a short stool to help me look at the saddle from front to back. Stand near the horse's shoulder and look through the pommel along the gullet toward the back of the saddle. See if the edges of the gullet are touching the horse's back. You can position your horse's hind end toward a light, or use a flashlight as a focal point.

Keep an eye out for "bridging," which is when just the *front* and *back* of the saddle are touching the horse. Also, look for the "rocking chair syndrome": just the opposite, it is seen when the *middle* of the saddle touches the horse's back, but not the front or back. This saddle will rock forward and back as you ride, especially at the canter.

Move to the horse's croup and look from back to front. Pay attention to the width of the gullet in relation to the horse's spine. When the gullet is not wider than the spine, its edges will constantly press on the spine, which "sores" a horse's back easily.

STEP THREE

The third step is adding the pad. If you show, use your show pad, otherwise use your regular pad. I always suggest people spend a little bit more money to get a pad made of quality material. The pad is important because of its location between the saddle and the horse's back: The higher the quality, the more comfortable the horse will be.

Review Steps One and Two to see if the pad changes anything in the fit of the saddle. Remember, if your saddle does not fit to begin with, adding pads will not improve it.

Now mount up, because your weight can change the fit—especially the saddle's levelness and clearance at the withers. Sit on the horse standing still (it is very important to sit in the correct position—see p. 61), and review the same areas as in earlier steps. Ride at a walk, trot, and canter. Don't think that because the saddle fits at the trot, it's going to fit at the canter. What usually happens is the saddle stays in place at the trot, and in the canter it starts slipping back or rocking.

Effects of Poor Saddle Fit

An ill-fitting saddle is uncomfortable and painful and will keep any horse from performing his best. When a horse exhibits such behavior as pinning the ears, switching the tail, "mouthing" the bit, flinching the skin, and/or getting "quick" in his gaits, you need to ask yourself, "Does my saddle fit my horse?" It's amazing how problems are solved by simply changing the saddle. Remember, using a pad or pads is not the way to fix a poorly fitting saddle.

Fitting the Saddle to the Rider

1. Wear your regular riding clothes when trying a new saddle.
2. Sit in the saddle with the correct riding position (see p. 61).
3. Check that the design of the twist (the front and center part of the seat) is comfortable—that is, it fits your pelvis.
4. Assess the length of your thigh. The point of your knee should end up somewhere in the middle of the knee roll on an English saddle. When you ride with shorter stirrups, your knee can be closer to the edge of the flap. In a Western saddle, you should have two to three fingers clearance between your upper thigh and the swell. English riders should check the length of the flap as well: you should have 4 to 6 inches of your upper boot in contact with the saddle.
5. Look at the seat size. Ideally, there should be the same amount of space—2 to 4 inches—between rider and pommel and rider and cantle. You should be able to sit in the seat with more of the cantle around your rump, not vice versa! Someone on the ground should do this measurement: Using two to three fingers, touch the back of the rider's rump and the top of the cantle. When only one finger fits in this space, the seat is too small; if four fingers fit, the seat is too large.
6. Finally, see how easily you can find the correct position and balance in all three gaits. If you jump, try the saddle over fences.

Bridles and Bits

Bridles

All of my schooling Western bridles have browbands because they stay on securely, though sometimes, I'll show with a "two-ear" bridle that is very popular in the show ring these days (see fig. 4.10 C, p. 72).

All English bridles should have a browband and cavesson (noseband) (fig. 4.10 A). The cavesson should always be snug, not tight: I like to be able to fit my

▲ *4.10 A–F* Train your eye by comparing English and Western bridles that are properly and improperly adjusted. Correct: A properly fitted English bridle and snaffle bit (A) and a properly fitted Western bridle with browband and throatlatch (B). Incorrect: A snaffle bit too wide for the horse's mouth (C); a curb bit too narrow (D); a snaffle bit adjusted too low (E); and a curb bit adjusted too tightly (F).

index finger in all around the cavesson, from the bridge of the nose and side to side. Its top should lie one inch below the horse's cheekbone.

English bridles always have a throatlatch: they are optional on Western bridles (fig. 4.10 B). When present, the throatlatch should be snug, yet loose enough to not interfere with the horse's breathing or movement. In the early nineties, I was in a dressage show riding a Quarter Horse called The Lark Ascending for one of my favorite judges. I finished my test, saluted, and after saying it was a very nice test he told me the throatlatch was a little bit tight. I thanked him and never forgot that when The Lark Ascending was fully collected with a "set" to his head, the throatlatch was pulling tight. That judge gave me a great tip.

Make sure your bridle is level and balanced on your horse's head by adjusting the cheek pieces to the same holes on both sides.

Bits

Whether a snaffle or curb, the mouthpiece should fit the width of the horse's mouth. When it's too wide, you can see the bit out of one or both sides of the horse's mouth. (fig. 4.10 C) Too small and there will be an indentation at the corner of the mouth (fig. 4.10 D).

When you adjust a snaffle bit or a curb bit with a broken mouthpiece for height, there should be one wrinkle of skin at the corner of the mouth. It should not "hang" where it can bang the horse's teeth (fig. 4.10 E). With a straight mouthpiece, the bit fits to the groove of the mouth with no wrinkle at all (fig. 4.10 F).

Be sure to look at the *diameter* of the mouthpiece in relation to the size of the horse's mouth. A horse with a shorter mouth generally likes a smaller mouthpiece. A horse with a longer length mouth is usually more comfortable with a thicker bit.

Curb Strap/Curb Chain

You need to be able to take your first two fingers and put them between the horse's chin and the back side of the curb strap or chain, and have the freedom to go from side to side on his chin. When you move the shank of the bit backward—bringing the curb strap in contact with the chin—the top of the bit that connects to the cheekpiece of the bridle should not fall forward. If it does, then your curb strap is too loose or your bit is too low in the horse's mouth.

With a Western horse I always start out with the less harsh *leather curb strap*, and then go to a chain if I need more response. All English curb bits have a "twistable" curb chain, which needs to lie flat against the chin.

Reins

I prefer leather reins because they lie flat in the palm of your hand and are pliable, manageable, and readily adjustable. I avoid lightweight, flimsy reins because

Bits: When Less Is More

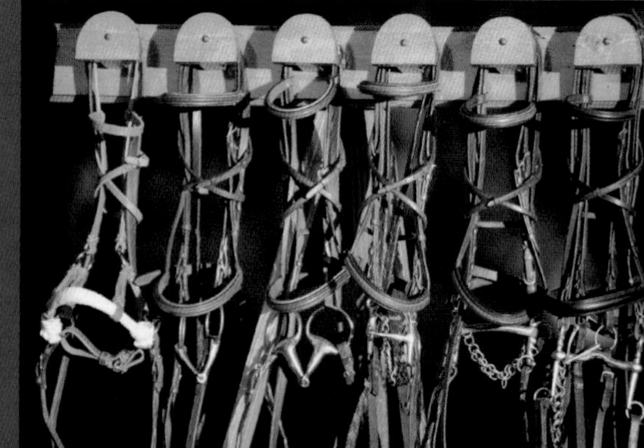

▲ *4.11* Learn how to judge the severity of a bit by its weight, diameter, and shape.

You can judge the severity of a bit by its weight, diameter, and shape. Lighter bits and larger mouthpieces are the least severe. When it comes to curb bits, lower and wider ports and shorter or curved shanks are kinder.

A lot of people think they need to use a more severe bit to get more response from their horse. But severity creates sensitivity, which in turn causes tension, resulting in the horse overreacting, or worse. When a horse knows what you want him to do—whether steer, slow down, give to the bit, or break at the poll—the more you stay with a "passive" bit the more you're going to be able to "work with relaxation." This is when I always get the most response.

they're too hard to keep organized, and thick or heavy reins because they are uncomfortable for me to hold.

Effects of a Poorly-Fitting Bit

The horse will give you a number of signs when he is not happy with his bit (fig. 4.12). Any type of quick action with the mouth means that the horse is frustrated, resisting, aggravated, or nervous. He may toss his head, gape his mouth open wide, or mouth the bit excessively. Horses generally put their tongue over the bit when it is too severe or too low in the mouth. However, these signs of discomfort may also be caused by problems with the teeth or be aggravated by the rider's hands. Have the symptoms evaluated by a veterinarian or use a video to assess the rider.

All of my young horses wear a bit for two to three hours a day. I position it low in the mouth, one or two bridle holes lower than normal, so the horse can put his tongue over it, under it, or whatever he wants to do to learn how to hold it. This is also beneficial for the older horse that mouths the bit excessively or habitually puts his tongue over the bit.

With some youngsters, I use a sidepull to start (fig. 4.13).

◀ *4.12* Poor-fitting tack can cause a multitude of behavioral problems.

◀ *4.13* Using a sidepull is less confusing or frustrating than a snaffle when a horse is learning his first walk, trot, and canter under saddle.

A Great Tip!

A habit I've had is to always check my tack before I get on. Make sure the bridle is *even* on the horse's head, and the bit, curb strap, and throatlatch are properly fitted. Review your saddle's position, tighten your girth, and then mount.

Training Devices

Running Martingale

A running martingale can be an effective training tool, especially for the young horse. However, many riders use one incorrectly as a device to get the head down and try to obtain a headset. A martingale should only be used in conjunction with your rein aids: you need to know how to get your horse to steer and give to the bit *without* using one first. If you do use a running martingale, only use it for a day or two at a time, every few months.

Draw Reins

Draw reins should always be used along with a normal set of reins (fig. 4.14). Unfortunately, some people—especially in Western disciplines—use draw reins by themselves, with a small, severe wire snaffle and attached to the girth between the horse's front legs, to try to get a headset. The horse evades this type of improper use by lowering his head and going on the forehand. This creates *false collection* (see p. 2).

Draw reins, like any training tool, need to be used with utmost respect and understanding. They can benefit certain horses at certain stages of training, but I feel they are devices best left to professionals who have the knowledge and experience to use them properly.

▲ *4.14* Draw reins should be used in conjunction with a regular rein to the bit, and only by riders schooled in their proper use.

Rider Aids

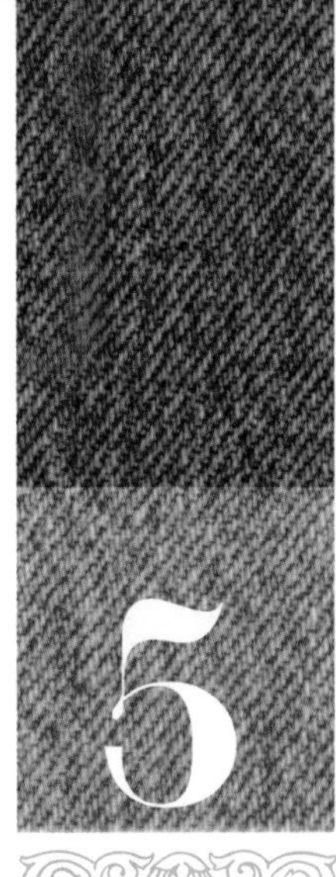

THE NATURAL AIDS YOU USE TO COMMUNICATE WITH YOUR HORSE ARE THE RIDER'S seat, legs, and hands (fig. 5.1 A & B). I discuss *artificial aids* a little later (see p. 84).

Natural Aids

First in the sequence of communication is the seat, which controls speed and is used to increase or decrease it through transitions. Second in sequence are your leg aids, which work with the seat as driving aids to *go forward*. Third are your hands, or the rein aids. When your horse has a confident knowledge of your aids, you should be able to use them with lightness. It is your responsibility to control your horse's balance by controlling his body alignment through your legs and reins, thus recognizing your horse's response to your aids.

Riding a horse from "back to front" is a simple concept when you understand what parts of your horse your leg and rein aids control. The legs influence the horse from the withers to the dock, which includes the back, barrel, hips, and hind legs. The hands control the forehand—the head, neck, shoulders, and front legs. Because the legs control a majority of the horse's body they are always used before the hands, which results in the horse being ridden from back to front.

◀ *5.1 A & B* Your natural aids—seat , legs, and hands—are used to communicate with your horse.

▲ *5.2 A–D* The rein effects: A left open rein (A); indirect rein (B); direct rein (C); and a right open rein and left indirect rein being used together (D).

Three Necessary Rein Effects

There are three different rein effects—*open*, *indirect,* and *direct*—needed to complete the training exercises in this book. The first two, open and indirect, are for all levels of riders and horses. The third, the direct rein, is only for advanced riders and horses.

With an *open rein* the rider's hand moves away from the horse's neck and opens sideways to achieve control of the horse's head position (fig. 5.2 A). The horse gives to this light pressure by flexing his head left or right, just enough so you can see his eye on the inside.

The *indirect rein*, which is an English riding term, is the same as the Western rider's *neck rein* (fig. 5.2 B). The horse yields from the pressure of the indirect rein against his neck. Do not cross your hand over the crest of the horse's neck.

A *direct rein* is when you make a fist with your hand on the reins and "hold" (fig. 5.2 C). In advanced training exercises, the direct rein is used primarily to turn without losing collection, especially at the canter. I use the direct rein sparingly, as there is a fine line between "holding" and "pulling." It is a subtle rein effect that can be quite effective with experienced horses when used correctly (fig. 5.2 D).

No matter which rein effect you are using, *never pull back* on the reins. The reins must be used *sideways*. Whenever you pull on the reins, you put a "wall" in

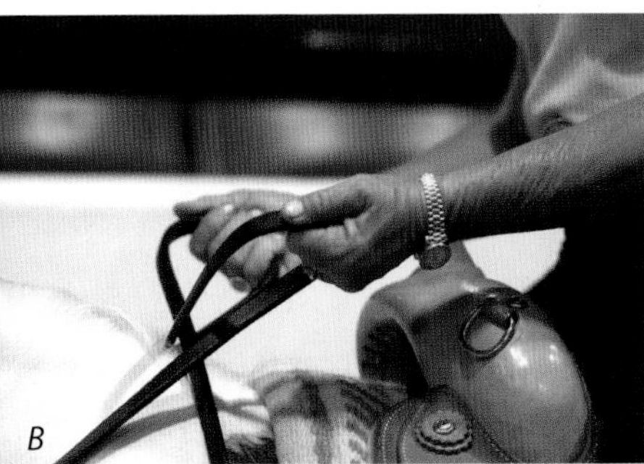

◀ *5.3 A & B* The correct position of your hands on the reins (A). To avoid pulling on your reins, turn your palms up, as though you were turning the ignition key in a car or unlocking a locked door (B).

front of your horse, blocking forward motion and giving him the perfect opportunity to lock, brace, and resist with his neck muscles, jaw, and mouth.

To avoid pulling, turn your hands so the palms are toward the sky, like the action of turning the ignition key in a car or opening a locked door (figs. 5.3 A & B). I tell my students to "turn the key" or remember my name, "Palm," and think "Palms up!" This action brings your elbows close to your sides and helps you learn to steer with a sideways action of the rein aids instead of what we naturally want to do, which is pull the reins toward our body.

Holding the Reins: Two-Handed or One-Handed?

Every training exercise in this book should be initially learned with two hands on the reins. Once your horse is confident in the exercise—and has reached the intermediate level (see p. 121)—you can begin to ride with one hand. It is more difficult to control the horse's forehand with your reins in one hand as opposed to two; it is also a coordination test for the rider that requires practice and preparation.

I like to start riding one-handed with split reins before advancing to romal reins. Split reins allow me to adjust my inside rein an inch to an inch-and-a-half shorter in the direction of travel, so I achieve the same rein effects in one hand—an open rein on the inside and an indirect rein on the outside—as I would with two hands. Similar to the English rider who switches to a full bridle in the advanced stages of training, a Western rider advances to a curb to improve the back-to-front connection while gaining lightness, enhancing roundness of the spine, and increasing uphill balance.

Rider Aids for Bending

Your *inside aids* are the primary aids used to bend your horse. The most active aid sequence needs to be inside leg to inside hand. As explained at the beginning of this chapter, the leg aid comes first (see more about leg aids on p. 83). When you apply pressure with your inside leg behind the girth, the horse should respond by moving away from pressure and starting to arch or bend his body. Your open rein flexes the head inward. Use an indirect rein if the horse tries to turn instead of just bending.

Your *outside aids* are active, supporting aids. The outside leg needs to be slightly farther back than the inside leg in order to support the bend by keeping the horse's hips inward—not swinging out. The outside indirect rein should lie against the horse's neck to keep the head from flexing too far inward or the shoulder from bulging out.

When you're on a curving line, not only do you have to bend your horse for balance, you have to turn the horse on that curving line. You turn with your *outside leg* and *indirect rein*, while your *inside leg* and *open rein* support the horse's bend, forward motion, and balance. For you to achieve balance, both legs and both reins have to actively tell the horse to control his entire body alignment every stride.

This is the foundation for creating a happy, willing horse. You must thoroughly understand the aids and aids sequence to control your horse's body alignment and straightness, and thus to achieve correct collection.

Rider Aids for Upward Transitions

The first and most important natural aid you use in transitions is your seat, followed by your legs, and then your reins. The seat is the most important because it is the least obtrusive aid. A stronger cue with the seat will not cause a horse to resist as he might with a stronger leg or rein aid.

Seat Aids

First, the seat is the aid that you use to increase or decrease speed and/or length of stride. As a rider you have to be in a nearly perfect position and balance. When you are sitting correctly on your seat bones, your hips will be tilted slightly forward, which allows them to freely move back and forth as you follow your horse's leg movements. When you correctly follow with your hips, you have the most comfortable ride and your horse is able to relax his back muscles, which makes it easier for him to lift his back as he engages his hind legs.

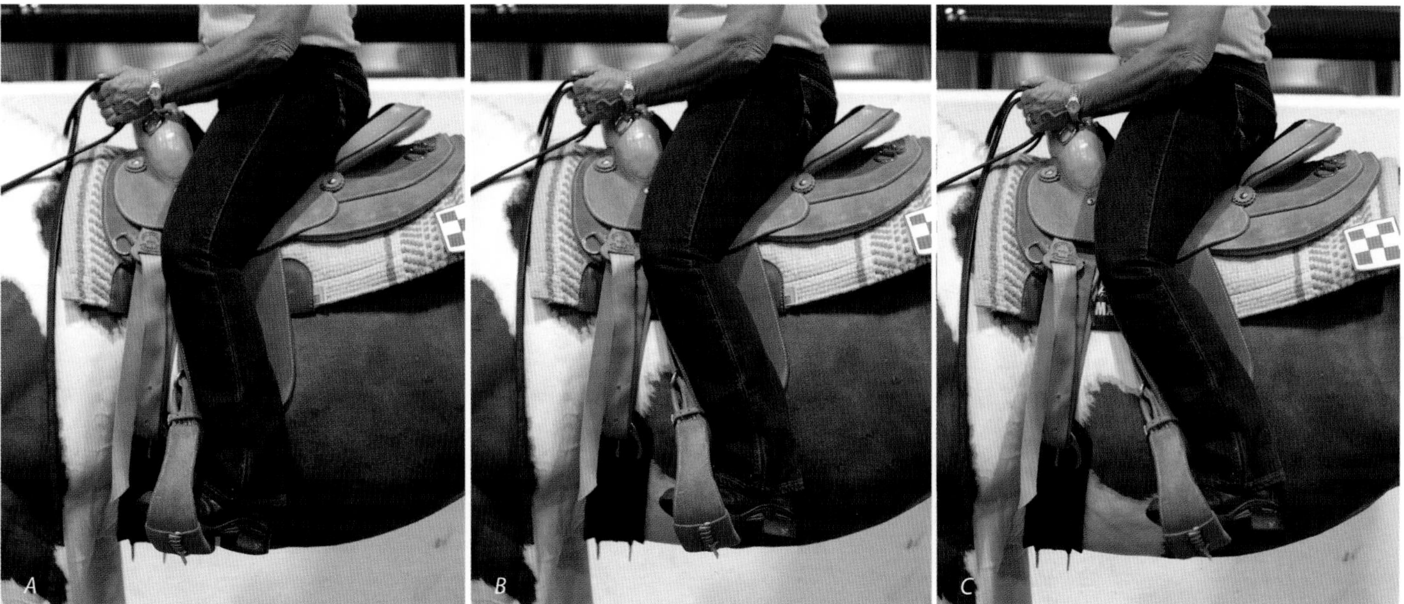

▲ *5.4 A–C* The rider's correct leg position is the first position used to apply pressure when communicating with the horse (A). Second position: You can move your leg slightly back to find a more sensitive spot on the horse's side and get a reaction, rather than squeezing harder in its original position (B). Third position: This is the furthest back you can place your leg without losing your seat. The rider's leg is in the middle of the barrel—*10* inches from the first leg position—and close to the hindquarters, which are controlled by the leg aids (C). You only use this position in training.

Horses feel a cue from a rider's seat through muscles that extend from the poll, across the topline, to the hocks. This allows a direct message to go from the brain to the hind legs of the horse, and is therefore a natural way to communicate with the horse.

In upward transitions at the walk and trot, as you move your hips forward, use the seat a little more assertively and "with thrust." For a canter transition, move your hips forward with a "scooping" action. The best way to describe it is the feeling you have when you are on a swing, and you push your hips in front of your body to make the swing go higher. Your seat action will be from the back of the saddle to the front.

Leg Aids

Your seat is supported by your leg aids. With your legs in the proper position just behind the girth, apply light contact with both legs to propel the horse forward for your walk and trot work (first position—fig. 5.4 A). When you quickly grip with your legs or just squeeze harder, you will get poor responses because you have given your horse the tools to ignore you.

▲ *5.5* I am demonstrating poor balance while looking down and using the spur incorrectly by lifting my heel and making contact too far up on the barrel of the horse. Note the worried and confused expression of the horse in his eye, ears, and tail.

Horses have a 10-inch zone from the heart girth to the middle of the barrel where they're the most sensitive. So if you don't get an immediate response, move your legs back slightly to find a more sensitive spot on your horse's side while still using light pressure, or add a light vibrating motion with your legs (second position—fig. 5.4 B). If you don't get a reaction after three tries, give the horse a whack with your leg to get his attention, and then immediately go back to asking with a light pressure (third position—fig. 5.4 C).

When your horse still isn't responding to seat and leg aids, there are three *artificial aids* for use in conjunction with your leg aids. You can use your *voice*, such as a cluck, to go forward. Also, a *crop* on the horse's shoulder can "wake him up" when needed, and when you're skilled in its proper use, a *dressage whip* behind your leg. An advanced rider can add *spurs*. All of these artificial aids *assist your leg aids* and are never your sole cue to ask your horse to go forward (fig. 5.5).

Rein Aids

Third in sequence for upward transitions are your rein aids, which are used to guide the horse. Slightly shorten your reins before each transition. This allows a good connection from your legs to your hands. With your reins you control the straightness of your horse's forehand, keeping the head, neck, and shoulders in line with the hips; or you can lightly flex the head right or left. You can slightly lift upward on the reins to help the horse lift his front end when he is too long in his body and/or heavy on the forehand (fig. 5.6).

◀ *5.6* Your rein aids are always used third in sequence to communicate with your horse. The seat and leg aids are so important that they can be used without rein aids at all, as I'm showing here without a bridle.

Rider Aids for Downward Transitions

For downward transitions, your seat works directly *opposite* of the way it does for upward transitions. You want to stop the movement of your hips by tightening the muscles in front of your hips—your lower abdominals—as well as tightening

▲ *5.7* Pulling on the reins puts a "wall" in front of the horse and gives him the opportunity to lock his jaw and resist with his neck and mouth.

your buttock muscles. Make sure your upper body and shoulders stay back and in line with your hips because the momentum of the moving horse will cause you to fall forward. Keeping your shoulders back will put more of your weight in the saddle, which helps the horse transfer more weight to his back legs.

Your legs should still be touching your horse's sides during downward transitions. This keeps his hind legs engaging and moving forward so he can slow down with power. You also use your legs to keep your horse's body and hindquarters straight, or "straight while bending" (see p. 87), during transitions of any kind.

Following the same sequence, use your hands to slow the motion of the horse by either closing your fingers on the reins or raising your hands slightly upward. *Do not* pull back on your reins by bringing your hands toward your stomach! You will get a "slow down," but you will also get resistance, as the horse can lean, pull up, or down, or go behind the vertical when your hands are fixed and pulling (fig. 5.7).

Straightness and Bending

Straightness

When a horse is straight and his spine is straight, then logically the horse's hind feet should be tracking where his front feet take off (fig. 6.1 A). Straightness, put simply, means the horse's hind legs track into the line of the front legs. In other words, the right hind follows the line of the right front, and the left hind with the left front. A horse also needs to be *straight while bending*, which means his body is not crooked and he is correctly bent on curving lines (fig. 6.1 B). In both cases, his spine corresponds to the line he is on.

Losing Straightness

My friend, trainer Al Dunning, describes a horse as being mechanically "bilateral." This means that when you bend one side, it affects the other. If you bring a horse's head to the left, his body—the front legs, barrel, hips, and hind legs—naturally go to the right. When you take his head to the right, his body goes left.

For instance, when a horse is walking on a straight line and swings his head to the right to look at something, the hind legs will track a little wider to the left than the front legs because his body bulges to the left and he becomes crooked. A crooked horse will always show signs of difficulty, stiffness, and resistance.

◀ *6.1 A & B* A horse traveling straight and balanced on a straight line (A), and a horse "straight while bending" at the canter (B).

Recognizing Straightness

Watch a horse move toward and away from you. On a straight line, you have to be directly in front or behind the horse, and a minimum of 10 feet away. On a curved line, watch the horse for about a quarter of a circle—coming toward you and going away.

You can easily see straightness by watching the footfalls. Are the hind legs in line with the front legs? Are the hind legs tracking to the inside or outside of the front legs? Once you identify straightness, or lack thereof, watch the alignment of the horse's body: notice his topline, and especially his head, eyes, and ears. Eventually, you'll be able to recognize straightness by the horse's body alignment and head position.

Straightness is balance. When you can control your horse's body alignment, you can control his balance.

▲ *6.2* Exercises on a curved line allow the horse to distribute more weight to his hind legs. Here you can see the left hind taking more weight while the right hind easily engages.

Bending

Bending, which supples the horse, is necessary for collection. Bending encourages the horse to engage or "use" his hind legs more, with more of his weight being transferred to them. When he's moving on a curved line, he has to engage the *inside hind leg* (fig. 6.2) to balance himself and be more powerful with the *outside hind leg* to keep himself on the curve.

Bending works the *lateral* muscles on both sides of your horse's body, from his neck, shoulders, and barrel to the hips. When a horse bends, the *inside* muscles are compressed and the *outside* muscles are stretched, which not only strengthens them but also supples them to allow the horse to move with fluidity.

It is a misconception that lateral suppleness is just bending the neck. When a rider just bends the horse's neck, it only encourages more weight to be placed on the *front* legs and doesn't do anything toward suppling the horse's body. Correct bending of the horse is flexing the head slightly inward and keeping the neck relatively straight.

To understand this yourself, lean forward while standing, letting your shoulders and arms hang down. Let's pretend you are the horse with your arms representing the horse's front legs. Turn your head left and right, keeping your head between your shoulders. Notice that your hands stay still—this tells you that in a comparable scenario the weight on the horse's front legs would not change.

Now, take your head and turn it all the way to the right, past your right shoulder. Your right arm lowers. So when the situation is transferred to the

Al Dunning on Collection

▲ *6.3* My friend, Al Dunning.

Al Dunning has been a professional trainer since 1970. His expertise in all facets of Western events has elevated him to great success in the American Quarter Horse Association, National Reining Horse Association, National Reined Cow Horse Association, and National Cutting Horse Association. Al has developed a winning tradition with Quarter Horses that is well documented. He trains, conducts clinics, and consults for ranch development and equestrian planning.

"When training for collection, I like to bend a horse by using my right leg to push his hip away with his head bent to the right," Al says. "Then I switch and use my left leg and 'push his hip into his head' as he goes. I like to be able to control all parts of the body with the head to the right and to the left. I feel I can control all parts of the body when the horse is straight. Straight is optimum when training a reining horse. Really, straight is optimum when training most horses. But straight doesn't mean *straight and stiff*. It means *straight and flexible*.

"One of the great faults in reining is when a horse falls out of lead in the circle. Let's say he's turning in a right circle. He's bending slightly to the right around the circle, and since his front is going to the right, his hip wants to go to the left. The horse will fall out of lead behind but stay in the correct lead in front, so he is cross-cantering. What we need to do is teach the horse to stay between our legs—*not* overbend him. The straighter he is the better, since it prevents him from making a fault because of his tendency to be bilateral.

"In cutting, we do a lot of 'go and stop,' where you push the horse up into the bridle with your legs until he flexes at the poll. When a horse flexes at the poll properly, he stays supple all the way through his spine to the tip of his tail, which keeps his hocks in the ground. When you can achieve this kind of collection and can run and stop and stay collected all the way through a turn, you'll have a shorter turning radius, which is quicker and can keep up with the cows we work today.

"No matter what you are doing, 'straight' is optimum, because the more 'bend' you put in that horse, the more he will revert to his bilateral nature."

horse, you see that more weight would go on that front leg. This is exactly what I *don't* want. The horse would have no option but to shift his weight forward and could shift his hips to the left, too. His ability to engage his hindquarters properly and to collect correctly would be taken away by bending the neck and pulling the head inward.

TRAINING EXERCISE 1: Circle Work

To get the most benefit from circle work, use cones to map out a circle of 70 feet (20 meters) in diameter. An easy way to accomplish this is to put a cone in the middle of your circle. From there, walk 10 to 12 large steps (approximately 30 feet) and set a cone, take two more big steps (approximately 6 feet) and put down another cone. Do this with four sets of cones—one set for each quarter of the circle—to create a track for you to ride on (fig. 6.4). Your goal is to ride the circle through the center of each set of cones.

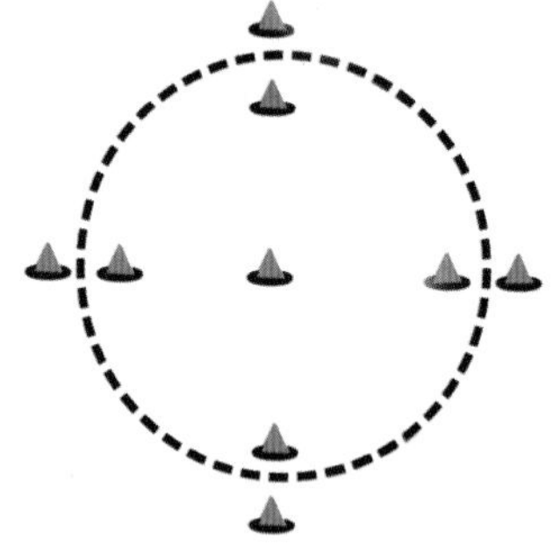

▲ *6.4* Four sets of cones create a center track for you to ride on a *70*-foot (*20*-meter) circle.

Practice using your aids correctly—riding leg to hand—to keep your horse bending (see p. 82). Start the bend by applying pressure with your inside leg behind the girth. Your horse should respond by starting to arc his body. Use your inside open rein to slightly flex his head inward. Support the bend with your outside aids: Your outside leg is slightly farther back than your inside to prevent your horse's hips from swinging out, while your outside, indirect rein keeps your horse's head from flexing too far in and his shoulder from bulging out.

When you come too close to the inside cones, either your inside aids need to be more active or your outside aids are too strong. When you come closer to the outside cones, your outside aids need to be more active or your inside aids are too strong.

The circle exercise helps you learn to recognize when your horse is in correct balance and control and when he loses his balance and control. Before you get to a weak area, whether it's falling out, falling in, speeding up, or slowing down, start reminding the horse how you want him to improve his response. If you don't recognize it, you can't improve it. When you recognize something but wait until the next circle to see if it is going to happen again, it's going to! A weak part of the circle will always be weak until you change it by improving the horse's balance and/or suppleness.

Use the cones to your advantage by looking ahead to the next set at each quarter of a circle. If needed, you can add four more sets of cones so you have eight sets altogether. Or try riding a circle without any cones, using your eye only to find the imaginary quarter point. No matter how you set up circles, try not to ride the same circle more than three times in a row: Change direction through the middle of the circle; ride a different figure; or stop and take a break. Circles can be very repetitive and your horse will get much more out of them if you ride two circles in one direction and two circles in the other direction, changing direction 10 times, than if you ride 20 circles in a row.

I remember training with Ms. Steele as a teenager on my summer vacation; the first three months were spent only training with circles. After we warmed up we went right to circle work. The goal was to learn how to get my horse balanced in both directions evenly on the circle, which also taught me how to ride a perfectly round circle. She kept the lessons interesting for me by explaining why something was correct or not. For the horse, she kept it interesting by changing direction and rewarding him for the smallest improvement. If he wasn't advancing we would stop, discuss why, and start over. Circles were my foundation for learning to collect naturally.

▲ *6.5* A horse falling in. I am trying to go on a circle to the left. The horse's weight is on his left legs, his head is to the outside and his shoulder and hips are moving to the inside. I am demonstrating using too much outside rein to turn and not enough inside aids to bend.

COMMON CHALLENGES

☛ *Falling in*: When you correctly bend your horse, you put the horse in balance. The most common loss of balance on a circle or curved line is *falling in*, which you'll sometimes hear people refer to as *dropping a shoulder* or *cutting in* (fig. 6.5). This loss of balance is similar to what happens to us when we trip and move more quickly to catch ourselves. The horse does this as well—he speeds up. Consequently, it's easy to tell when he is no longer bending correctly on that curving line.

When a horse flexes his head to the outside of the circle, he leans inward with his inside shoulder and inside hip to balance. This is falling in. The way to correct it is to get the horse to move out. He needs to yield his body away from your inside leg, start bending his body again, and move wider on the curve.

To achieve this, apply your inside leg, and use your indirect inside rein to flex his head inward and yield the forehand outward. Should you get little or no result, you must not get stronger with

▲ *6.6* A horse falling out. The head is flexed too far inward with the neck bending, and the shoulders and hips are swinging out. This is a common problem when a rider tries to bend or turn using mostly the inside rein.

your hands—something I commonly see. You actually cause the horse to go even more *inward* when your inside rein aid becomes stronger than the inside leg aid. Once he's back in the correct bend and balanced, soften your aids.

☛ *Falling out*: The second most common loss of balance on the circle or curved line is when the horse goes too wide or falls out (fig. 6.6). This happens when his head comes too far in, the neck bends and the shoulders and hips swing out. Usually, it's from a rider using way too much inside rein to either bend or turn the horse. To correct this on a circle to the left, first use your right leg; you want his body to come back in onto the track. Then, you want the horse to yield from your right indirect rein and straighten his head and neck. Once you get him back in on the track, support again with your left leg and rein to ride a balanced curve.

▲ *6.7 A–C* Start with a balanced, happy horse on a curving line (A). I'm looking ahead to the straight line coming up. While still on the curve, I start to straighten the horse (B), and by the time I reach the straight line, my horse is balanced and straight (C).

TRAINING EXERCISE 2: Curving Line to Straight Line to Curving Line

To control your horse's balance riding from a curving line to a straight line, you need to be able to straighten your horse's body position. A long oval is the best training figure to practice such an exercise.

When you are curving to the left and want to go straight, your aid sequence controls your horse's body alignment (figs. 6.7 A–C). When in a correct bend going to the left, his hips are slightly to the left (inward). First, use your left leg aid to straighten his body. His head is also flexed inward, so use your right open rein to straighten the head. These *diagonal aids*—left leg and right rein—straighten the horse. As he becomes straight, use both legs and both reins evenly to maintain his straightness.

When on a straight line going to a curving line, you need to bend your horse before you actually turn him on the curve (figs. 6.8 A–D). Prepare at least 12 to 24 feet ahead of the curve when on a young horse, less with a more experienced horse and/or rider. The sooner you start bending your horse in preparation for the

▲ *6.8 A–D* When riding from a straight line to a curve, keep your horse stra ght and balanced (A). Prepare for the curve by starting to bend your horse while still on the straight line (B). You can see the tip of my horse's right ear as his head flexes slightly inward and his body starts to bend. As you begin the curve, your horse is ready with the correct bend to his body (C). At the end of the Straight Line to a Curving Line exercise, your horse should still be balanced and happy (D).

Training Figures

Different figures—for example, circles and figure eights—can be ridden as a warm-up, as the goal of a training lesson, or in cool down. They can also be used in every exercise you practice. Riding figures makes you think about how to be effective and keeps your horse interested in his schooling session while improving his responses and fitness level. The more often you change direction, the more you work with the lateral suppleness of your horse, and the more transitions you ride, the more you develop the horse's topline muscles and strengthen his hind limb joints.

These training figures are included throughout the book and are found as follows: changing direction from a straight line (p.95); figure eights (p.109); small circles within a large circle (p. 111); three-loop serpentines (p. 126); half-volte (p. 150); and loop on both long sides (p. 152). As I mentioned before, variety is important in any training program and I use these figures with every horse whenever I train or warm up for competition.

curve, the more time you have to use your aids in the proper sequence, and the longer your horse has to comprehend and respond to your aids.

COMMON CHALLENGES

☛ *Wiggling or leaning:* A horse that "wiggles" through a straight line is usually exhibiting a lack of forward motion. When you are working at the walk, try the same exercise at the trot, or increase speed within the same gait. Encourage your horse to go forward to improve straightness. It's harder, though, to improve your horse's straightness when slowing down.

When a horse isn't traveling straight, he can be leaning either to the left or right—you feel him get heavier on your leg and rein aids on one side or the other. If this is the case, focus your eyes on a spot ahead and try riding a straight line to it. Or use two cones and try to ride a straight line between them in a dirt riding area. Look at your horse's tracks in the dirt: His footfalls will tell you if he is leaning or straight.

Training Figure: *Changing Direction from a Straight Line*

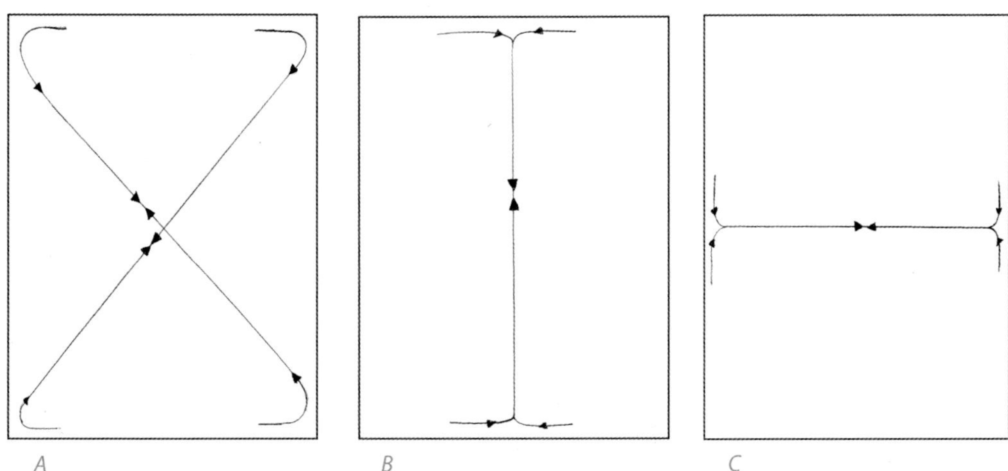

▲ *6.9* A–C. Changing direction on the diagonal (A); on the length of the arena (B); and across the width of the arena (C).

There are three ways you can change direction in an arena for this exercise (or others): On the diagonal (fig. 6.9 A); on the centerline along the length of the arena (fig. 6.9 B); or through the width of the arena (fig. 6.9 C). These three figures improve your horse's *straightness while bending*. They offer tighter turns than circles making them more challenging to ride correctly and precisely.

TRAINING EXERCISE 3: Spiraling Out and In

Spiraling out is an excellent exercise for bending and suppling, and to teach the horse to give to the inside rein and come on the bit using the back correctly with more engagement from the hindquarters (fig. 6.10). For example, if a horse is pulling, beyond the vertical (also known as "nosing out"), or flat through his body with no roundness to his spine, I like to use spiraling-out training exercises on a circle.

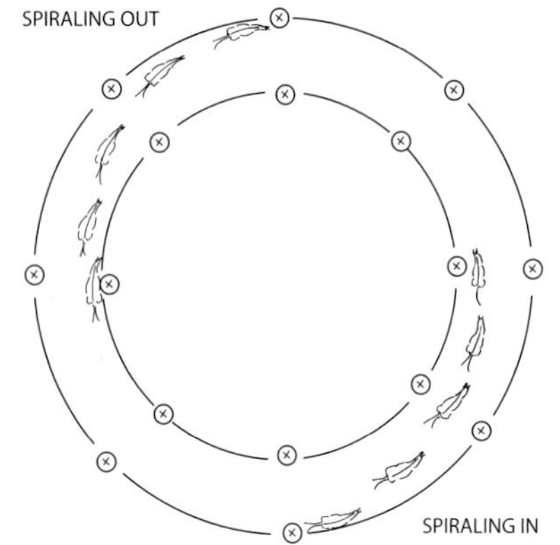

▲ *6.10* Spiraling out and in.

Start with your 70-foot (20-meter) circle and four sets of cones at each quarter (see p. 90). Place the two cones that form your riding space 10 to 15 feet apart so you can now fit three tracks within these cones—the middle, the outside, and the inside distance.

To start spiraling out to the left, ride the middle track of the circle. After you go through a set of cones, gradually make your curving line wider so that you finish on the outside track at the next set of cones. Encourage the horse with your left leg to give to the left indirect rein to move outward. As you are moving outward, your outside aids (right leg and rein) must support the bend and straightness, as well as keep the horse spiraling out slowly. The spiral should be gradual enough so the horse does not change his rhythm, body position, or balance.

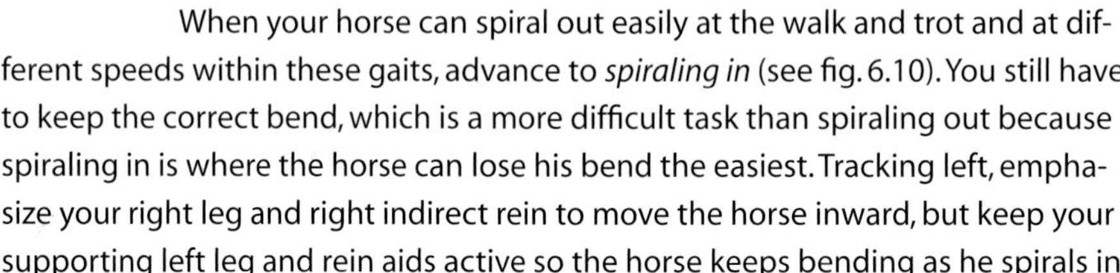

When your horse can spiral out easily at the walk and trot and at different speeds within these gaits, advance to *spiraling in* (see fig. 6.10). You still have to keep the correct bend, which is a more difficult task than spiraling out because spiraling in is where the horse can lose his bend the easiest. Tracking left, emphasize your right leg and right indirect rein to move the horse inward, but keep your supporting left leg and rein aids active so the horse keeps bending as he spirals in.

When your horse does the exercise easily and correctly at the walk and trot, you can advance to the canter. The spiraling exercise teaches him to respond lighter to your aids, connect from the leg aid to the rein, become supple through bending, and encourages him to move in an uphill balance.

COMMON CHALLENGES

☛ *Horse spirals too quickly:* The biggest challenge riders face when spiraling out and in is when a horse moves too quickly, which prevents him from getting the full benefit of the exercise. As the rider, you must keep the horse moving gradually outward or inward. Keep your *supporting aids* active, as these slow down his response to your dominant aids, and keep him *straight while bending*. Make sure you recognize and keep the horse in the correct bend while doing the spiral out or in, for when you lose the bend, you lose balance, straightness, and rhythm.

When you want your horse to consistently follow a path or regulate his speed, your aids must be active and maintained every stride. Many beginner riders cue their horse to do something, then do nothing until the horse isn't steering or moving correctly, then they'll cue again and let go again. It's a huge advancement of riding skills when you can communicate with your horse every stride. When you understand which parts of the horse your aids control and can use both legs and reins at every stride, you can ride your horse precisely, and when he is balanced he will be willing. Our goal working with horses is to achieve willingness, which makes us happy because our horse is happy. This is what horse training is all about!

TRAINING EXERCISE 4: Canter Poles

This exercise is a great way of improving your horse's canter; however, make sure that you can do it at the trot first (fig. 6.11). If, after you have progressed to canter find you have difficulty, go back to the trot and improve at the slower gait.

Start by placing one pole—at least 10 to12 feet long—on the ground and canter over it. When you can canter the pole in stride, it means that you're controlling your horse's body alignment, balance, and consistency of rhythm. The horse shouldn't change any of these qualities before the pole, over the pole, or after the pole.

Add a second pole on a straight line at a set distance. Always measure from the *inside* of one pole to the *inside* of the next pole. The horse's natural canter stride is anywhere from 6 to 9 feet. Have someone on the ground to watch and help change the pole distance slightly to match your horse's natural length of stride. You want to make it easy for him to be successful at the exercise.

I like to have at least one stride between the two poles to make it easier for the horse to keep his balance. For example, set the poles 12 feet apart, canter over the first one, land, take one stride, and canter over the second pole. You can widen the distance by adding 12 more feet to get two strides between the poles. The goal of the exercise is to control the horse's balance and regulate a steady rhythm and speed.

A key factor to this exercise is the rider's eyes: When you look down at the poles, you can easily break the rhythm and be late with your aids to keep your horse's balance and straightness. You must look out *beyond* your next pole. You can also add cones to ride between. These will either assist in maintaining straightness or help you recognize when you are losing straightness.

Once the horse performs well over two poles, add more poles on a straight line. When he does very well with at least four poles at different distances, advance

to a curving line. I like to use the Circle Exercise (Training Exercise 1, p. 90) and put a pole between the set of cones at each quarter. Make sure that you start with one pole, then two, and master three, before doing four poles. When you can ride four poles, you are riding your horse in a controlled rhythm and correct balance.

COMMON CHALLENGES

☛ *Horse breaks gait:* The most common problem in this exercise is when the horse breaks to a slower gait. To avoid this, you must be more active with your driving aids—your seat and legs (see p. 82). On the other hand, when your horse speeds up, use your seat and rein aids in perfect timing to regulate his speed. You don't want to "shut the horse down" suddenly and break gaits.

☛ *Horse is not straight*: When your horse strays off the line, it changes the perfect distance between the poles, thus making it harder for him to take each pole in stride. When this happens, use the cones to keep him straight.

☛ *Horse hits the poles:* Any time you are having difficulty at the canter, go back to the trot. With any ground pole training, when your horse hits a pole with his toe or the front of his hoof, you are going too fast. When he hits it with his heel or steps on top of it, you are going too slowly. A ground person or video can help you here. When you keep the same rhythm and speed, and control your horse's straightness and balance, you will not hit any poles.

◀ *6.11* When your horse is balanced on a curve he will take a ground pole in stride and keep his balance before, over, and after it.

Beginning Training Exercises

In following chapters I include my general training exercises for various stages of training. With each training exercise, I discuss one or two commonly faced challenges, although each horse teaches us something new.

After a horse has a strong natural carriage under saddle (see p. 28), developing a rounded, uphill-balanced, collected horse is accomplished first, through transitions; second, by suppling muscles and encouraging more weight onto the hindquarters through bending; third, through longitudinal balance, which stretches and compresses the topline muscles; and fourth, through lateral work. In chapters 7, 8, and 9, I incorporate each of these four elements, based on the horse's stage of training.

The exercises in this chapter are for what I like to call the "beginner" horse—a horse of any age that has never been trained for collection. Generally, a beginner horse is younger and just starting collection work, having had the opportunity to learn natural balance and carriage under saddle. This is such an important part of my successful training program. A horse must learn to carry a rider, in any gait, and remain balanced according to his conformation and relaxed when viewed from the profile.

However, older horses can be beginner horses, too, and learn about collection for the first time. A horse that has been trained in "false" collection can also restart his education. I am a firm believer that you can retrain horses—that is, teach older

◀ *7.1* An important part of my training program is for the horse to learn to carry a rider, in any gait; remain balanced according to his conformation; and appear relaxed when viewed from the profile.

horses new things. However, more than likely there will have been some damage done—mental and behavioral—if a former rider used some of the techniques I described at the beginning of the book (see p. 6). In such a situation, the horse learns to be defensive, and this can be difficult to overcome.

With all beginner horses, train with patience: Let your horse tell you when he comprehends an exercise and can accomplish it easily and consistently. Then he is telling you he is ready to move on.

TRAINING EXERCISE 5: Simple Transitions

Transitions are the first steps taken to teach your horse how to transfer more weight to his hind legs, engage the joints in his hind end, and round his spine, which compacts his body in the way necessary for him to be collected. The flexibility of his hind limb joints—hip, stifle, hock, and fetlock—is increased. Transitions also work on the suppleness of his longitudinal muscles; they stretch when the horse goes forward and compress when he slows down, which builds strength and enables him to go forward and slow down with more power.

An *upward transition* is a change from a slower to a faster gait, or from a shorter to a longer length of stride within the same gait. To cue for an upward transition use your seat more assertively; add a light contact of your legs behind the girth; and slightly shorten your reins to connect your horse from your leg to your hand (see p. 82).

A *downward transition* is a change from a faster to a slower gait, or from a longer to a shorter length of stride within the same gait. Downward transitions also start with your seat by stopping the movement of your hips without falling forward. Your legs remain in contact with your horse's sides while your hands slow your horse by gradually closing your fingers on the reins or slightly raising your hands (see p. 84).

Riding on a *curving* line encourages a horse to engage his hind legs because he has to bring the inside hind leg deeper underneath his body for balance while the outside hind leg pushes off with more power. Consequently, a horse slows down when doing transitions on a circle. Start by riding a 70-foot (20-meter) circle and practice:

- Halt–walk–halt
- Walk–trot–walk
- Trot–canter–trot

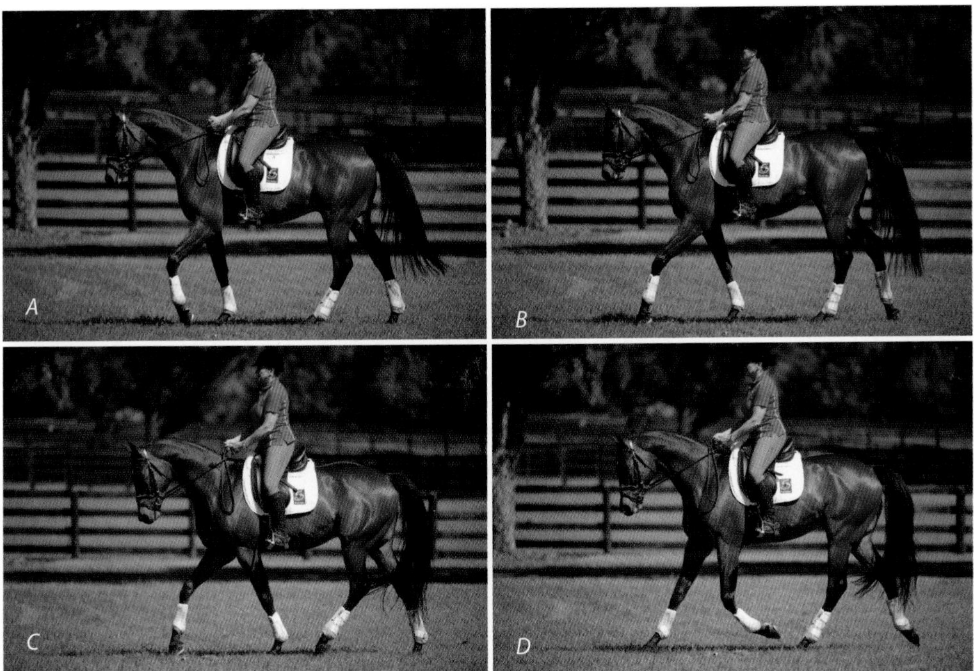

▲ *7.2 A–D* For a transition from walk to trot, start by controlling the speed of the walk and straightness of your horse's body alignment (A). Use your seat and leg—the driving aids—to ask your horse for the upward transition (B). Continue to use your rein aids to maintain your horse's straightness as he begins to trot (C). When you have a balanced transition you will easily have control of speed and direction in the new gait (D).

Halt–Walk–Halt / Walk–Trot–Walk

HOW TO

For the *halt–walk–halt* transitions, start with your horse standing straight and square. Ask him to move in an active, forward, marching, four-beat walk for one full circle, halt for no more than five seconds, and walk off again. When your horse stops straight and smoothly, and walks off instantly and still straight, you can advance to halting at each half circle, then each quarter circle.

Follow the same pattern as you move on to the *walk–trot–walk* transitions (figs. 7.2 A–D). Walk one full circle, perform a transition to the trot and continue trotting for another full circle, then return to the walk. The trot should be an active, square trot, where the hind legs track in line with the front legs, with your horse bending correctly (fig. 7.3).

▲ *7.3* My horse and I enjoy this ride at the trot on a loose rein. He is straight but there is no connection from back to front, he is not engaging his hind legs and is flat in his topline. He is going in his natural carriage without giving to the bit or flexing at the poll, both of which are needed for the horse to be collected.

COMMON CHALLENGES

☛ *Horse not straight and forward:* Because forward motion is slower, the walk is the hardest gait to ride. When your horse is not connected from your leg aids to your hands, he will weave his head and not go forward, or move left or right and not go straight.

If your horse moves to the left, for example, as you ask for a transition, perhaps he is reacting to a too strong leg aid. Most people have one dominant leg that is stronger than the other—my right leg is stronger than my left. Simply use less right leg and more left leg aid together with your seat. This is the common way to correct your horse's responses during transitions in any gait.

Natural Mechanics

I like to describe uphill balance as being similar to a speedboat on water (fig. 7.4 A). When the boat is not moving, it is level with the water. But when the boat accelerates (just as when the horse increases his speed or lengthens his stride) the back of the boat goes down because it gets its power from the motor, which is in the back, and the front of the boat lifts up. That boat would not go anywhere if the front end were to dive into the water instead. It would sink. It's similar with a horse on his forehand. When more weight is carried by the front legs instead of the back legs, he's not going to go forward very easily.

When the boat's speed is reduced, the motor pushes the back of the boat down and elevates the front, so it can slow down quickly. When a horse slows down with more weight on his front legs, the stop is going to be jarring and rough, and it will certainly be met with resistance from the horse through your reins. A horse must slow down—with power—like the boat: from behind while elevating his front end to achieve a smooth downward transition or stop (7.4 B & C).

A

B

C

▶ *7.4 A–C* At the collected trot, you can easily see an uphill balance (A). As my horse slows down to a halt, he continues to bear more weight on his hind legs and less weight in front (B). As a result, the horse stops in a way that is physically easy for him. Note his square legs, which tell you that he is straight and balanced (C).

◀ *7.5 A–C* The trot–canter transition is initiated first from the seat, which you move from the back to the front of the saddle in a scooping motion (A). To take the left lead, cue with your right leg aid, as it controls the right hind leg of the horse, which is the first beat of three for the left lead canter (B). When you have a slight bend to the left in a left lead canter, your gait will be fluid and your horse relaxed (C).

Trot–Canter

Canter transitions require you to use your aids in a slightly different manner: Your seat is used in a scooping action from back to front in the saddle (fig. 7.5 A); your inside leg creates a light bend to the horse's body in the direction of the lead, while your outside leg cues for the canter; and both reins steer, while the inside rein flexes the horse's head slightly in and the outside rein supports straightness.

HOW TO

To create the correct, balanced position for a left lead canter departure, your left leg has to be in contact behind the girth for the horse to bend his body around as well as to prevent him from falling in when you ask for the depart. Your right leg is held further back than the left leg and is used to cue your horse in conjunction with the action of your seat for the canter departure. Your outside leg controls the first beat of the horse's three-beat canter. Going to the left, the outside right hind leg of the horse (you cue with your right leg) is the first beat in the canter (fig. 7.5 B). The second beat is the footfall of the horse's left hind and right front legs together, and the third beat is the horse's left front foot as it hits the ground to complete one stride.

Your left open rein, or sometimes the left indirect rein, controls the horse's forehand and flexes the horse's head inward just enough so you can see the horse's eye while the neck slightly curves with the shoulders (fig. 7.5 C). Your right indirect rein has contact against the horse's neck so his head cannot go too far inward and the right shoulder doesn't fall out. This is the same rein-aid sequence you use to bend your horse (see p. 88).

To initiate the canter, your seat, both legs, and both reins have to actively establish the gait and control the horse's body position *during* the transition. Many inexperienced riders position and cue their horse, then quit riding as they wait for the horse to canter. A smooth transition is the sign of a rider who has light and effortless control of the horse's direction and balance before, during, and after any transition, especially the most difficult canter transition.

Remember, for a horse to make a balanced canter departure his body has to be slightly bent in the direction of the lead. Never bring the head to the outside and "throw" the horse into the lead. This only causes future problems. At the beginning, you can use a corner in an arena, a curving line through cones, or poles on the ground to help. Let the obstacle encourage the horse's natural bend and allow you to introduce the canter transition with light cues.

COMMON CHALLENGES

☛ *Rider's reins are too loose:* Sometimes, a rider who is focused on properly using the seat and leg aids forgets to maintain contact with her rein aids during an upward canter transition; or an inexperienced rider loosens her reins to "help" her horse into the faster gait. A horse needs light rein contact from both reins to help him round his back as his hind legs engage the canter. When the rider loosens the reins, the horse flattens his back, shifts more weight to the front legs, and doesn't canter. He will trot faster every time. If you keep a connection from your legs to your reins during the transition, you will be successful—and obtain your first steps of collection!

☛ *Horse hurries through transitions:* When retraining an older horse, you have to experiment and decide which transitions need to be improved. If he hurries or falls in during an upward transition, encourage him to take his time. Use a curving line for the transition, position your leg aids, and make the horse wait for your cue.

Sandy Collier on Collection

Sandy Collier has enjoyed great success in her career as an NRCHA, NRHA, and AQHA champion horse trainer. To date, she is the only female rider to win the world's toughest cow horse event—the NRCHA World Championship Snaffle Bit Futurity, which she did in 1993 on Miss Rey Dry. In 2002, she was AQHA World Champion on Sheeza Shinette.

"To achieve collection, I do a lot of work through speed and gait transitions, which makes no sense at all to most reining or Western riders," says Sandy. "Even though we get them real collected at the trot and lope, we really have to work them up to some speed to run down the fence. No matter how collected your horse is, as soon as you start putting a lot of speed to it, it's like the wheels start falling off the car. One of the things that I do is called the Runaround (fig. 7.5 B).

"I'll build speed while maintaining collection for a long, straight run. As I approach the end of the arena, I'll take a deep breath, start to exhale, and make my horses follow my seat as I sit down in the saddle, making them come back to me on a straight line without falling out of lead. It's like downshifting a real expensive car, where it has to come back down real smooth. Once you get around the corner, build speed again and start over. My horses eventually get to where they can run really fast while staying collected, and then as I let my air out, they'll come all the way back to a slowdown or a stop, depending how long I sit.

"Lots of horses have a low 'do-not-exceed speed.' By pushing up to that speed, then backing off it and making them collect up and soften, then nudging up to it again, we can desensitize the horses to going fast. Every horse can get a higher do-not-exceed speed, but some can stay balanced and in control while going faster than others. The Runaround is an exercise I've done forever that has definitely stood the test of time in my barn."

▲ *7.6 A* Sandy Collier trains horses that excel at the world's toughest cow horse events.

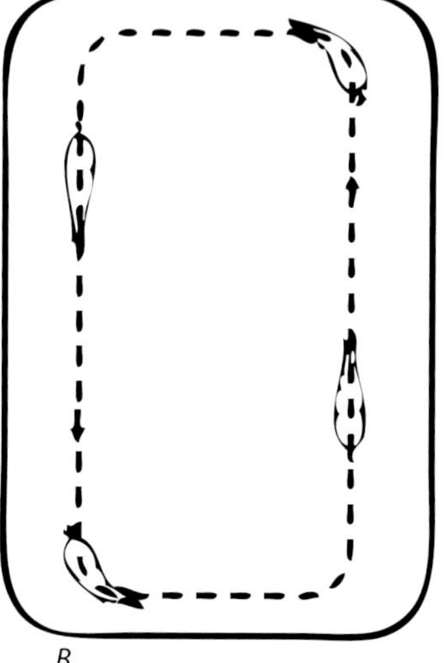

◀ *7.6 B* This exercise improves the quality of your horse's rundown, which in turn improves the quality of his stop. Practice this exercise in the middle third of the arena, at least *20* feet from the fence. Simply build speed down the long side, then sit deep in the saddle and pick up your reins to "downshift" and slow down at the end of the straight as you approach the turn to the short end. While on the long side, be sure to slow down to the speed you wish to ride the short side—don't let the horse careen around the corner. Keep your horse slow and collected through the short end, and ask him to build speed gradually again down the next long side. Work equally in both directions.

If he does the transition as soon as you position your legs, slow down to the trot and try the transition again. At the trot, keep your legs in the canter position until he relaxes and holds his bend, then ask for the canter.

Canter–Trot

To go from canter to trot you use the same aids as for every other downward transition: Stop the action of your seat while sitting deep in the saddle, keep your legs on your horse's sides to help keep him straight and his hindquarters engaged as he slows down, and close your fingers on the reins or slightly lift your hands upward to slow your horse (see p. 84). It is especially important with the beginner horse that he makes the downward transition when *you* ask for it, not when he wants to.

For most horses, either upward transitions are a little easier than downward transitions, or vice versa. Use commonsense and understand your horse's natural instincts. For instance, a more sensitive horse will have an easier time with upward transitions but need more time for slowing down. When your horse is the anxious type, stay in an enclosed area and use a curved line for downward transitions to naturally improve control. A more docile horse needs more time to perfect upward transitions, while downward transitions are attained more easily because he *wants* to slow down. When your horse is lazy, you can work outside of the arena (see "Think Outside the Box," p. 110) or do upward transitions on a straight line to encourage forward motion.

Training Figure: *Figure Eight*

This an excellent figure for doing transitions in a straight line, after and before changing direction. It is especially helpful if your horse loses his balance, leans, or changes speed. The curves help you rebalance him so you can improve the next transition on the straight line.

When people first ride a figure eight, the first quarter- to half-circle is usually smaller than the second half. Use cones to define your figure eight training: Ride the center track between cones set 3 to 6 feet apart at each quarter to make your figures uniform (see fig. 9.18, on p. 165). If you need help on the straight line, use cones set 3 feet apart to make a "chute." Your circle will be round when you consistently control your horse's body position. (For other Training Figures, see the sidebar on p. 94).

COMMON CHALLENGES

- *Falls on the forehand:* A horse can easily fall on his forehand when the rider

▲ *7.7* The horse is falling on the forehand, a common challenge in downward transitions. Note my wide, fixed hands positioned below the crest of the neck, setting the horse up to evade pressure on his mouth by lowering his head.

uses the reins first to slow down (fig. 7.7). The horse shifts his weight to the forehand and pushes against the rider's hands instead of using his back and his hind legs to slow down.

When your horse falls on his forehand in the canter–trot transition, review your own aid sequence. Make sure your legs are in contact with the horse's sides as you use your seat. This encourages the horse to keep his hind legs going forward, engaging under his body. Also, use your reins in an upward motion. This allows him to slow down naturally in an uphill balance.

☛ *Transitions are abrupt:* When your horse makes an abrupt downward transition, you want him to do it in slow motion, so to speak. You want to "elongate" the time he takes to slow down so he has plenty of time to keep his balance. Keep him on a curving line, as this naturally slows a horse. It doesn't always have to be a circle, you can send him forward and go straight or do a figure eight, but when you ask for the downward transition on a curving line, it encourages the horse's weight and balance to shift to the hindquarters. If he starts to drop his head down or fall on the forehand, send him forward and try again.

Think Outside the Box

When a horse isn't "thinking" forward, sometimes all you need to do is take him outside the arena (fig. 7.8). Get him outside of the "box"! The new environment will increase his sensitivity level—and thus response time—because he isn't stuck looking at the same surroundings. You will get more forward motion, which can be exactly what a lazy horse needs to excel at upward transitions or learn to respond to light aids.

◀ *7.8* If you want to keep your horse happy while training, school him outside the arena!

TRAINING EXERCISE 6: Lengthening Transitions

As I mentioned in chapter 4, a horse should be proficient at the walk, trot, and canter before training for collection. You should know how to ride three speeds within those gaits—a natural, lengthened, and shortened length of stride (see p. 102). If you have prepared your horse correctly, he will already be comfortable and consistent traveling at his natural length of stride. Then, I always train and perfect lengthening of the stride before advancing to the more difficult shortening of the stride (covered in chapter 9—p. 145). Lengthening the stride preserves the correct cadence and quality of the gait.

When you start to teach stride lengthening, some horses get worried, quick, and hurried in their mind. It's hard for them. You have to spend the time to get them comfortable to where they can lengthen, not lose their balance, and keep thinking "slow." On a curving line, start with the walk and trot, and practice these transitions:

- Natural walk–lengthened walk–natural walk
- Natural trot–lengthened trot–natural trot

HOW TO

When you're in a natural length of stride and want to lengthen, don't change your upward transition aid sequence. Start with your seat increasing its action, close your legs, and shorten your reins, keeping slightly more contact than before. Compress your horse in an uphill balance and keep him straight to allow his hind legs to engage and his shoulders to open and reach forward to lengthen the stride.

To return to a natural stride, use the same aid sequence as a downward transition: your shoulders stay back to add more weight to your seat, your hips stop moving, your legs stay in contact, and your reins are used in an upward action to maintain an uphill balance while slowing down.

Use the time between transitions to prepare for the next one. Your goal is to keep the horse in front of your legs and moving with positive energy, engaging from behind. When the horse is in a correctly, balanced position, he can smoothly and energetically lengthen his stride in a gait.

Training Figure: *Small Circles within a Large Circle*

This is my favorite training figure (fig. 7.9). I like to use a 70-foot (20-meter) circle for my large circle, and ride smaller 35-foot (10-meter) circles inside of it. I use this figure to improve upward or downward transitions as I complete the smaller

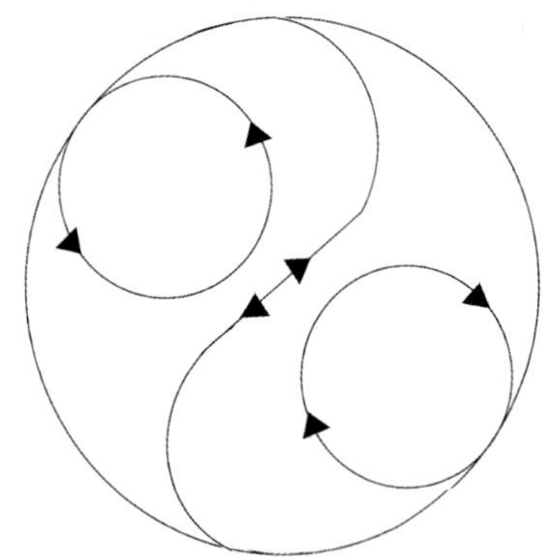

▲ *7.9* Smaller circles within a large circle.

circles. The figure helps the rider be more aware of the horse losing his balance and is a beneficial tool for changing stride length between the two different-sized circles. For this particular exercise I would use a lengthened stride on the larger circle and a natural stride on the smaller circle, although in other exercises, you could also canter the larger circle and trot the smaller, for example.

Changing direction through the middle of the circle can be tricky. Divide the circle in half, and choose your path before you change direction—it should resemble an "S." When you change, sit and bring your inside shoulder back for the tighter turn, quickly straighten the horse's body position, look ahead to the new direction, bend the horse in the new direction, and turn him on the circle. Try to accomplish the change of direction without a loss of rhythm or energy. (For additional Training Figures, see the sidebar on p. 94).

After practicing on a curving line, try these transitions on a straight line. When you are in an arena, try to keep your straight line at least 10 feet off the rail. The rail can be a useful reference point for straightness, however, you will be forced to use your aids more actively to keep your horse straight if you do not rely on it for guidance.

COMMON CHALLENGES

☛ *Horse's stride too quick:* Your goal is to lengthen while keeping a steady rhythm and tempo; however, a common problem is the horse just goes faster. This usually means your reins are too loose. And an abrupt change of speed instead of a gradual lengthening of stride means you are asking too much with your legs. There has to be a connection from your seat and legs to the reins to get a longer stride, giving you more speed but not a fast and "running" stride.

TRAINING EXERCISE 7: Transitions between Poles

Accomplishing accurate transitions between ground poles requires you use your driving aids and be light with the reins. It also asks the horse to be responsive right away, not be lethargic, and maintain the correctness of his body position and alignment—that is, stay balanced and straight. If your horse is light and responsive to your aids in this exercise, he is in front of your leg (see sidebar, p. 113).

Putting Your Horse in Front of Your Leg

"Putting your horse in front of your leg" means that your horse responds immediately and with lightness to your driving aids—your seat and legs—and has a desire to go forward. In all of the training exercises used to achieve collection, your horse has to be "thinking" forward and constantly responding to your legs. Simple upward transitions—halt to walk, walk to trot, and halt to trot—on a curving or straight line are excellent exercises to put your horse in front of your leg.

If you ask your horse to go forward and he is sluggish, exhibiting a delayed response, problems will arise in your attempts at collection. You must create more energy for a horse to be able to collect. Putting your horse in front of your leg encourages him to engage his hind legs. This gives you the necessary power and impulsion so you can ride him from "back to front" (see p. 2).

There is a quick and simple way to test if your horse is "thinking" forward: After you make an upward transition, gradually take your legs off the horse's barrel. If he slows or shuts down, or loses his forward impulsion, he is not in front of your leg. When he stays at the same speed, your horse is "thinking" forward.

HOW TO

Place a series of poles on the ground with 24 to 48 feet between each one (fig. 7.10). The longer the distance between the poles, the more time you have to perform the transition. The shorter distance is for the advanced horse and rider. Don't hurry transitions. Set the distance that allows you enough time to use your aids accurately and gives the horse time to concentrate on what you are asking. As your ability increases, you can advance the exercise by setting the poles closer together, or on a curving line.

Work on the following transitions:

- Walk–halt–walk
- Walk–trot–walk
- Trot–halt–trot

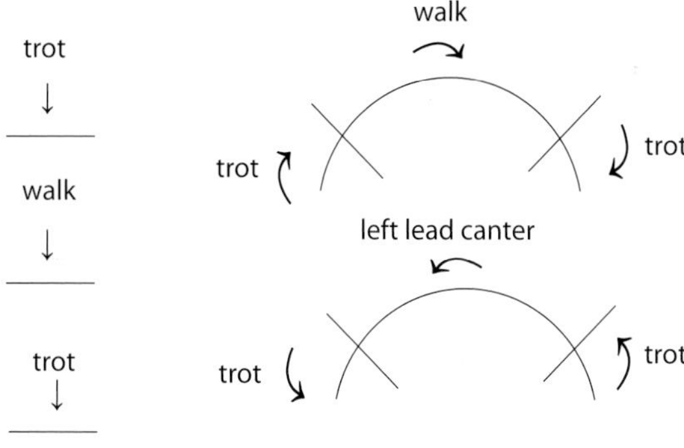

▲ *7.10* Sample transitions between poles.

- Natural stride trot–lengthened trot–natural stride trot
- Natural stride walk–lengthened walk–natural stride walk

Be precise. Stay on the line you set, whether it's straight or curving, and make sure your horse responds within the planned distances.

COMMON CHALLENGES

- *Horse's forward response is delayed:* If you ask the horse to go forward in an *upward* transition to a new gait or for a lengthening of stride and he delays for three or four strides, do not just keep on going. Assess your horse's straightness and his concentration, and stop using the ground poles. Return to the speed you started with and ask for the upward transition again, adding a quick kick with the legs or a nudge from your crop or spur to "wake him up." You want him to respect your command. When you get an improved response, reward your horse and return to the pole exercise.

Remember, after an improved response, stop and praise the horse. This ensures you will have a willing horse ready to try the exercise again or advance. Short segments are extremely important to keep your horse's concentration and responsiveness. After this simple exercise, let your horse walk and stretch his back by loosening the reins. Keep the walk active. Give him lots of strokes on the neck, too!

▲ *7.11* Your reins are not to pull on! Pulling gives the horse an opportunity to resist and puts more weight on his forehand.

- *Rider pulls on the reins:* A commonly seen challenge in this exercise is pulling on the reins to ask for downward transitions (fig. 7.11). The horse responds by slowing down, but your action gives him an opportunity to resist by pulling forward against your hands and bracing his neck muscles, jaw, and mouth. A horse that pulls has more weight on the front legs and less on the hind legs. You're giving the horse the opportunity to "run through your hands" because you've taken away from him the necessary mechanics for him to slow down correctly.

Review the proper aid sequence—seat, legs, hands (see p. 79). Naturally, we all want to use our reins first, but remember, it's *seat, legs, and then your reins*! And when you use the reins in an *upward* manner, you encourage the uphill balance your horse needs in order to be collected without giving him the opportunity to pull or resist. If you are not getting a quick downward transition, assess the straightness of your horse's body position. When he is straight as you are requesting the transition with the correct aid sequence, he will slow down immediately.

TRAINING EXERCISE 8: Turn on the Forehand

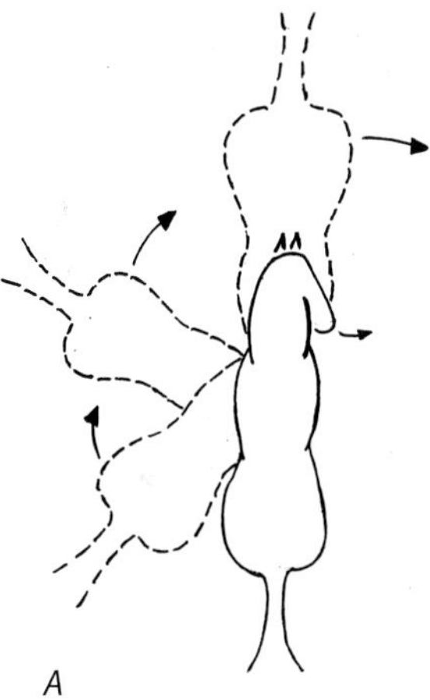

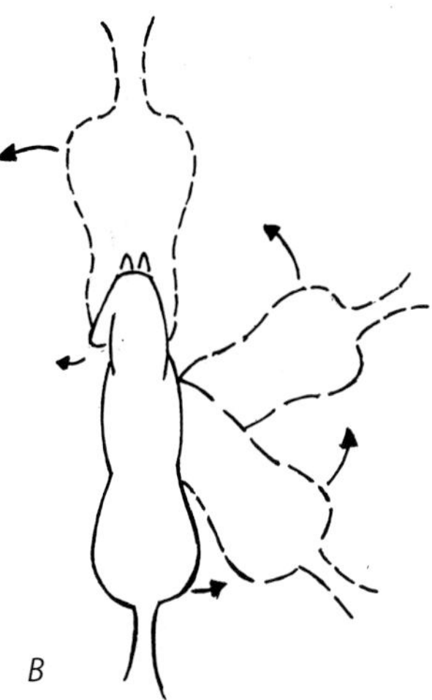

▲ *7.12 A & B* Turn on the forehand moving the hindquarters to the left (A) and to the right (B).

Lateral training maneuvers are accomplished in three ways: moving the horse's *hind legs sideways*; moving the horse's *front legs sideways*; or moving the *front and hind legs sideways at the same time*. These training exercises improve the horse's coordination, strengthen and supple the horse's muscles through the sideways movement, and increase the flexibility of his joints, especially in the hind legs. Sideways movement also encourages the horse to put more weight onto the hind legs, which as you know transfers some weight off his front end.

Lateral exercises progress in difficulty. The easiest is the turn on the forehand, where the hind legs move sideways around the front legs, which stay almost still (figs. 7.12 A & B). The horse's body alignment is straight. These lateral steps taken by the hind legs are the first *yielding* steps the horse learns.

HOW TO: ON THE GROUND

To begin, I teach the turn on the forehand from the ground so I do not confuse the horse. Use a fence as a guide for straightness. Stand your horse parallel to the fence, and move to his offside, between the fence and your horse—you should be standing on your horse's *right* side ready to move his hips to the *left*.

Position yourself at the horse's shoulder and stretch your right arm straight to hold the horse's halter. Take his head slightly to the right, toward your body. Because the horse is bilateral (see p. 89), this will cause his hips to go left. Position your left hand in a fist just behind his heart girth, slightly below the middle of the barrel, where your leg aid will eventually be. Do not look at your horse's feet! Look at his topline, as straightness of his body position is a must for success of the maneuver.

Ask the horse to move away from pressure on his barrel by moving his hips to the left. Your right hand at the halter will keep your horse straight and not allow any backward steps. Maintain his straightness as the hind legs move sideways to keep the front legs relatively still. Complete a 180-degree turn and walk the horse out of it, keeping your left fist on his side until you walk forward.

▲ *7.13 A–C* For a turn on the forehand to the right, the horse's hips move to the right (A). This is your foundation movement to teach a horse leg aids as well as to control the hindquarters and forehand independently. The turn on the forehand is the first lateral training movement. Notice the horse's hind legs move sideways, crossing the left in front of the right when the hindquarters move to the right (B). The right indirect rein keeps the front legs from moving to the right. The right leg aid keeps the horse "thinking" forward (C).

Remember, the movement is for the horse to learn to move away from pressure on his side, so you can't do it from the halter bending the neck—you will sacrifice straightness. Be sure to follow the horse's motion with your fist and keep a constant light touch. An on-again-off-again touch on his side could aggravate or confuse him—tail switching might be an indication.

HOW TO: UNDER SADDLE

To accomplish a turn on the forehand moving the hindquarters to the right under saddle: 1) Make sure your left leg stays in the correct position on your horse's side approximately 2 inches behind his heart girth; do not bring your heel up—cue with the calf of your leg (figs.7.13 A–C); 2) use an indirect right rein against the neck to keep the front legs from going right; 3) put your right leg just behind the girth to keep his body alignment straight; 4) use the left rein to flex the horse's head slightly to the left, which will swing the hips to the right.

The turn on the forehand is a useful maneuver to maintain a young horse's concentration as you take a break from trot and canter work, for example. It is also beneficial for teaching a rider how to coordinate leg, rein, and light aids. However, once performed well, the turn on the forehand should not be used over and over, because it encourages more weight to be carried on the forehand. Instead, advance the training to *yielding* (see below).

COMMON CHALLENGES

☛ *Rein aids are too strong:* When doing a turn on the forehand to the right, riders tend to use the left rein as their strongest aid instead of their left leg (and vice versa). When they do this, they flex the horse's head to the far left, bend the neck, and bring the shoulder to the right of the hips (fig. 7.14). The horse has to respond to the left leg to move the hips to the right. Remember, the indirect right rein keeps the forehand and shoulders straight in line with the hips. The right leg stops the movement, as well as maintaining straightness.

Horse walks forward: When your horse wants to go forward, that's okay. Just close your fingers on your right rein to stop him. It is more important that he doesn't decide he wants to go backward. If he backs up, you're using too much rein at the start or during the movement, or you need to be more active with your leg aids.

▲ *7.14* This horse is not straight therefore cannot perform a correct turn on the forehand. I am too strong with the left rein and not active enough with the left leg, and also not supporting with the right rein.

TRAINING EXERCISE 9: Yielding on a Diagonal Line

After your horse has mastered the turn on the forehand, it is time to teach *yielding*, which can be done in three ways: on a *diagonal line*, which I deal with here (fig. 7.15); on a *straight line* (see p. 136); and on a *curving line* (see p. 138). Yielding teaches the horse to move his front and hind legs together in a forward lateral step. As with the turn on the forehand, I teach yielding from the ground before doing it under saddle.

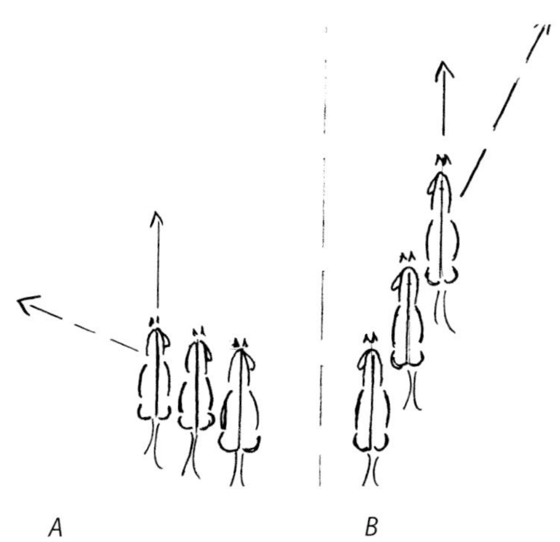

▶ *7.15* Yielding on a diagonal line: On the left, you see yielding to the left with too much angle (A). This makes it difficult for the horse to stay forward. Yielding with less of an angle, as shown on the right, is the easiest way to train yielding on the diagonal (B).

I like to use the fence as a guideline to teach this exercise. When the horse learns what to do, you can do it anywhere. When you are working in an arena, first divide it lengthwise into half and then into quarters. Start on a quarter line and yield diagonally to the fence, making a gentle angle of approximately 15 degrees. Later, you can advance the exercise by starting at the centerline and yielding your horse toward the rail at an angle of approximately 30 degrees.

HOW TO: ON THE GROUND

Let's yield to the left. Position yourself at the shoulder on the horse's off- (right) side. Open your arms, with your right hand on the halter and left fist positioned on the barrel where your leg would be when riding. If your horse immediately moves when you touch his barrel, start your touch at his neck and gradually move your fist to his barrel, as if you were brushing or petting his side. Your right hand at the halter keeps the horse forward and straight at an even speed.

First, walk forward and straight for at least three to five steps. Bring your horse's head slightly to the right and to move him sideways, add a light steady or pulsating pressure with your left fist. Coordinate your left hand in time with your right hand to ask for the forward-and-straight body position and sideways (diagonal) movement. Do not look at the horse's feet! Look where you want to yield, and at the horse's topline. When you keep your horse's body position straight, as with the turn on the forehand (see p. 115) the horse will move both sets of legs laterally on a diagonal track.

Be sure you don't control the movement from the halter, which could cause the horse's shoulders to move ahead of his hips. Straightness is the key. When you and your horse master this exercise on the ground, and you have perfected the turn on the forehand under saddle, you are ready to *yield on a diagonal line* under saddle.

HOW TO: UNDER SADDLE

Just as you did on the ground, start by walking forward on a straight line. When your horse's body alignment is straight, ask him to yield on a diagonal line to the right: 1) Apply pressure with your left leg to yield his body to the right; 2) use an indirect right rein to keep his forehand straight and in line with his hips; 3) support with your right leg to keep his body straight and maintain even, forward steps; 4) flex his head to the left with an indirect left rein to encourage his forehand to lead the movement (figs. 7.16 A–C).

If you get two or three lateral steps, stop and reward your horse. Give him the opportunity to understand what you're asking and the positive reinforcement to want to try again.

▲ *7.16 A–C* To start yielding, first go on a straight line track. To yield to the right, the horse's head should be flexed slightly to the left (A). This horse is straight and correctly balanced as he yields to the right (B). He can move his legs laterally to his fullest capability (C).

When your horse can yield at the walk from a quarter line to the rail down the length of the arena, increase the slope of the diagonal line—from centerline to rail—to get more lateral movement. The straighter you can make your horse, the more he can cross his hind legs as much as his front legs, and maximize his lateral step. Take the time to develop this, as it is his first lateral movement with both front and hind legs together. There are many other lateral movements for advancement, and you want your horse to excel at this exercise before you move on.

COMMON CHALLENGE

☛ *Horse gets crooked:* You'll find the same challenges with yielding as occurred with the turn on the forehand. For example, when the left rein overrides the other aids when yielding to the right, the horse becomes crooked. He will lead with his shoulder too far in front of his hips, and proper yielding cannot be accomplished. Remember, you also have to stay balanced in the center of the horse to feel straightness for your horse to respond to light aids.

Intermediate Training Exercises

A horse is ready to move on to intermediate exercises when he is relaxed; confident with his ears pricked forward; responding well to your aids without the addition of your voice, crop, or spurs; and happy in his work, not resisting you in any way. Moving from beginning to intermediate exercises can be the toughest time in your training progression because your horse now will have to use additional muscle to physically compress his body as he rounds his spine more. The horse has been able to move in a free, relaxed natural carriage, and now you're starting to manage his body position and balance, and asking him to react more to your aids.

It is really the hardest stage to go through, and can result in inconsistencies. Your horse may have some temper tantrums along the way, where he balks at going forward, goes too fast, leans on your leg aids, tosses his head everywhere, and isn't accepting of your hands—in general, just disobedient. Ride outside of the arena and refresh him, then come back and do it again. If you can get one improved response, let it be. Sometimes you just have to ride a horse through these arguments.

The reason it is so hard to start training your horse for collection is you have to build his muscles and develop flexion in his joints. This takes time! But if you continue to put the horse in a correct body position, and continue to ask for a round frame, you will get willingness very soon. You need to be patient—and assertive—as you develop the horse's body.

◀ *8.1* Transitions at markers can help improve your horse's response to your commands.

Be aware of the difference between a horse throwing a tantrum because he's being asked to do something more difficult, and one who is not physically or mentally ready to move up to the intermediate exercises. When you progress too soon, your horse will struggle with the new work. He'll be trying, but he will have difficulties: He might be sluggish, surge, get crooked, mouth the bit, switch his tail, or grind his teeth.

When he's not doing something well, go back to a simpler exercise, even if it means spending extra time on the beginning exercises. You have lots of simpler lessons to review in order for the horse to regain his confidence. Give him more time to concentrate and "slow his mind down." You will gain his willingness and have a better chance of success advancing him later on.

TRAINING EXERCISE 10: Long and Low (Giving to the Reins through Bending)

For a horse to be able to be collected, learning to give to the rein and flex at the poll is vital. A horse that goes "flat" in his back and his balance, pulls, or gets heavy in the reins, or one that raises his poll to evade rein contact has to learn to stay connected—that is, "on the bit." The horse is connected "over his back" so energy created by the rider's legs travels from his hind end to his front and "into" the rider's hands. This is the first step toward teaching the horse to break at the poll. A horse in a long-and-low balanced frame with a "rounded" spine, giving to the bit, and with his head beyond the vertical, is in the first stage of collection.

HOW TO

The long and low training exercise should start at the trot on a curved line. While riding on a curved line with contact on both reins, raise your inside hand straight up 6 to 12 inches. Keep contact with the mouth as the horse raises his head or pulls against the rein. Actively use your inside leg for your horse to give to the pressure from the rein. When the horse feels the upward rein tension, it is difficult for him to keep his head up, especially on a curved line. The goal is for him to give to the bit by lowering his head and neck. If he yields slightly outward on the line you're riding, that's okay. Maintain your outside leg and rein aids to support his bend, and don't let him lose his balance and fall out or the curve could become bigger and wider (figs. 8.2 A–D).

As soon as you start to feel your horse give to the rein you must *release* and lower your hand to follow his head downward back to a normal rein position—but do not lose the contact. Also, don't let him yield outward on the curved line anymore. With both leg aids, encourage him to drive forward from behind, which

▲ *8.2 A–D* If your horse is not giving to the bit, raise the inside rein with slight pressure on it(A). Move your inside leg back and actively use this leg aid to get your horse to give to the inside rein. As the horse starts to give to the bit, lower your hand while keeping a light contact (B). Continue to follow your horse's head with your hand as he stretches down (C). Your horse will end up in a long-and-low, balanced frame, having correctly given to the bit (D).

will give him the long-and-low balance. Continue with even contact to the bit with both reins, thus allowing your horse to be comfortable in your hands and support his balance and rhythm. You won't actually go faster, you'll just cover more ground and achieve an elongated stretch.

While this exercise is mostly done at the trot, you can do it at the walk and, when more advanced, at the canter. No matter which gait you choose, the horse should keep the same steady rhythm. When your horse is in a long-and-low balance, he raises his back up and rounds it by stretching his topline muscles. This allows him to swing his hind legs deeper underneath himself. A fit horse in natural carriage can do this exercise easily and willingly. Younger horses, or horses in the earlier stages of collection, need to be built up slowly. Start with a 70-foot (20-meter) circle, asking your horse to go long and low for one quarter of the circle.

▲ *8.3* This horse is in a correct uphill balance in a long-and-low, balanced frame. Although the left rein is loose, the horse is bending properly on a left curve and is straight from the contact on the right rein.

A horse can go long and low and still maintain a correct balance (fig. 8.3). This is the balance for hunter under saddle, or any discipline where the horse needs to move with his head and neck in a more level position. The head can be beyond, or on the vertical, the poll and neck in a level position, or slightly above the withers. Older, more finished horses enjoy the long-and-low position as a warm-up exercise: It supples their muscles and gets them ready for collected work.

COMMON CHALLENGES

☛ *Rider's timing at the release:* Some riders have difficulty at first finding the perfect timing and releasing their hand as the horse's head goes down. It is important for the horse to understand that when he gives to the bit from your leg aid, he is immediately rewarded by you lowering your hand. Try to follow his head smoothly as you lower your inside rein. Make sure there is no "on-and-off" contact, or jerking, or you will lose the horse's acceptance.

☛ *Reins are too loose at release:* If you let the reins go loose as your horse gives to the bit, he can bring his head back up, or shorten and quicken his stride. When this happens, reestablish contact, take him onto a curved line, connect him from your leg through to your hands at a trot, and ask him again to give to the bit and lower his head and neck. However, be sure his poll never goes below his withers or his weight and balance can move more onto the forehand.

TRAINING EXERCISE 11: Stretching Down

Stretching down is important for the horse's development at the intermediate stage of training. Stretching at the "free" walk is a scored movement in lower level dressage tests, and considered so important, its score is doubled. The judge is looking for a horse that wants to stretch his body as long as possible, and the lower he can stretch down with his head, the more he will stretch his back and hindquarter muscles.

For a horse to do this correctly, he has to be connected from back to front and in an uphill balance, so when you loosen the reins, he'll follow the reins downward and stretch down willingly.

HOW TO

As you ask the horse to stretch down, use your legs to encourage him to elongate his stride without increasing his speed, giving him the maximum stretch. Make sure that you bring him back on the bit slowly to encourage him to connect and round his spine again. Increase your leg pressure as you shorten your reins and bring him back connected and in an uphill balance.

Stretching down is a physical development exercise, as well as necessary for giving a horse a break from being collected. I might ask a young horse to stretch five or six times in a lesson.

COMMON CHALLENGES

☛ *Horse doesn't stretch:* If a horse is in false collection, more than likely he will not have as good of a stretch, or won't stretch at all (fig. 8.4). He might lengthen his body and stick his nose out, but he will not stretch down with the head and truly exercise the topline muscles.

☛ *Horse inverts the topline:* When you loosen the reins, your horse could invert, or hollow his back. This happens when the horse has been in false collection (see p. 2) with his head just set in a position or being ridden from front to back. Use Training Exercise 10: Long and Low, to encourage the head to lower and stretch. You have to be patient, stretch only a little at a time, and continue to connect and round your horse with new exercises. You must keep him straight and balanced in order for him to be able to stretch out his back.

▲ *8.4* A poor example of stretching down at a walk on a loose rein. Although the horse has lengthened his body and is long and flat, not much stretch is happening and he is on the forehand.

TRAINING EXERCISE 12: Intermediate Transitions

After you have mastered the simple transitions in the last chapter (see pp. 101–111), add these more difficult ones:

- Trot–halt–trot
- Trot–halt–back up–trot
- Trot–canter–trot
- Natural canter–lengthened canter–natural canter

Training Figure: *The Three-Loop Serpentine*

The serpentine is a valuable figure for transition work (fig. 8.5). Like the figure eight (see p. 109), the three-loop serpentine involves changing direction, but because you're changing direction more often and in a shorter period of time, it can be more difficult. The smaller your curving line and the shorter your straight line, the more difficult the figure. You can add more loops for a higher degree of difficulty.

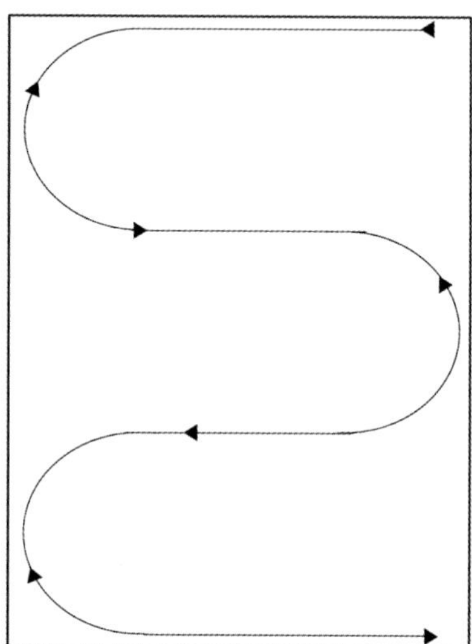

▲ *8.5* A three-loop serpentine.

As you practice your transitions on the serpentine, try to keep your half circles and straight lines of even size and length. Otherwise, it becomes uneven and your horse loses his rhythm. The key is to—in advance—assess the size of the area you are working in and decide where you are going to make your half-circles and the size they need to be for correct bending and turning. Getting your horse straight at the end of each half-circle helps you stay on course. If you struggle, use cones as a guideline. Three sets of cones on each half-circle and one set in the middle of the straight line will be all you need. (For more Training Figures, see the sidebar on p. 94).

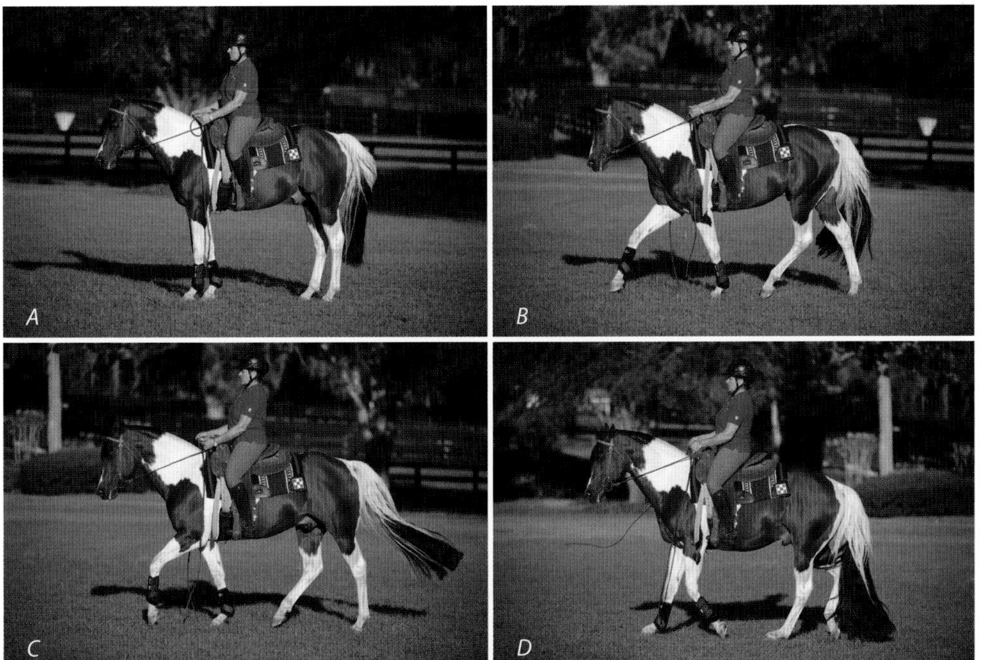

▲ *8.6 A–E* Make sure your horse is standing straight at the halt (A). Keep the timing to a minimum so your horse doesn't relax too much, or he may have difficulty moving forward into the trot without any walk steps. Your goal is to have your horse engage with power while keeping an uphill balance (B). Keep a connection from your leg to your hand as you continue in the trot (C). To ask for the halt, stop your hips from moving; keep your shoulders back and in line with your body; maintain your leg contact on your horse's sides to keep his hind legs moving forward; and use your hands in an upward action (D). Here you can see a perfect example of uphill balance while slowing down (E). By keeping your horse straight through the transition you will get an immediate, willing response.

Trot–Halt–Trot

HOW TO

For the horse to be in front of your leg, a great training exercise is a trot-halt-trot transition. First, establish a working trot, and halt. Your goal is to achieve a stop while standing absolutely straight with your horse's weight on all four of his legs. Ask him to trot again. When your horse is standing straight and square, you will get the *desired* response—that is, a trot with no walk steps. Trot for five to 10 strides and halt again (figs. 8.6 A–E).

With an *average* or *poor* response, just trot for two or three strides and try again. An *average* response means the horse gets a little crooked, takes one walk step, or raises his head and neck to pull himself into the trot, indicating not enough hind leg engagement. A *poor* response includes several walk steps, leaning one direction or the other, stopping crookedly, or inverting his topline. Straighten the horse through the walk as you're doing the downward transition to the halt so you can improve the next effort. Halt for no more than three seconds—the longer you wait, the more chance your horse has to relax and become dull before going forward.

The trot–halt–trot transition is an excellent test of whether or not your horse is in front of your leg (see p. 113) because it requires the horse to engage his hind legs more than he does in the walk to trot transition.

Trot–Halt–Back Up–Trot

HOW TO

This transition sequence also requires the horse's hind legs to engage more. With your reins, ask for him to back up by closing your fingers and lightly lifting your hands. Don't pull the reins toward your stomach. As soon as your horse starts backing, relax the reins without releasing, and keep a light pressure on them. If he slows his backing motion, add more rein pressure in a give-and-take action by slightly opening and closing your fingers; avoid a steady rein pressure because your horse could pull against it. Your legs should be touching the horse's sides and keeping his hindquarters going straight. You can back a horse with the leg aids, but make sure you don't confuse him by using too much leg pressure, which would be like stepping on the gas and putting on the brakes at the same time.

Begin this exercise by backing up one or two steps, then asking for the trot. You must achieve straightness in order to be successful. As with the trot–halt–trot transition (see p. 127), immediately return to the halt if you don't get the correct response. Work up to three to five steps of backing up and five to 10 strides of trotting. End the exercise when you have at least three to five good transitions in a row. When your horse gets stronger, you can advance the exercise with more transitions.

COMMON CHALLENGES

☛ *Horse overreacts during backing up to trot transition:* Many "hotter" horses have too much energy, making this upward transition difficult. When your horse darts forward, it could be because he overreacts to the leg cue. Your natural reaction will be to take your legs off his sides, but avoid this impulse because when your legs are off and you cue him again, it will be even more jarring to him than the first time. I liken it to getting a static electricity shock without warning, as happens from our cars in the winter. This is what it feels like to your horse.

You need to teach the horse to accept leg contact. Do this by desensitizing him. While standing still, massage your leg on the horse's side, touching him continuously. Do one leg, then the other, then both legs together, swinging them back and forth on his sides. He may move at first, but when he will stand still, you have desensitized him to the touch. Do the same procedure while walking the horse. He has to learn to accept the feeling of your legs, and once he does, he will love it and you will obtain positive, smooth transitions. When you have a horse a bit insecure as well as sensitive, contact from your legs can give him confidence.

Trot–Canter–Trot

In the intermediate stage, the trot–canter–trot transition progresses from the more basic version you learned in chapter 7 (see "How To" on p. 106). Now, you begin to ask for a little more bend to your horse's body, and ask him to respond more quickly to your seat and leg aids through transitions— consistently and without any effort. The trot–canter–trot transition, really for me, is the transition that I have to perfect—without any crookedness, resistance, or loss of roundness—before I move on to the more advanced form of the transition, which is shortened trot–canter–shortened trot (see p. 147).

Don't move on too soon. At this intermediate stage of training, you should not continue to the next stage of any transition unless it is perfect or near perfect. A transition is like putting your car in gear. When you shift smoothly and correctly you have complete control of the speed. When you shift gears badly, you'll have trouble with the car's speed for a while. A correct, balanced transition from one gait to another allows you to keep your horse in control, and control is necessary for maintaining correct collection.

COMMON CHALLENGES

☛ *Horse picks up the wrong lead:* When the horse changes his body position from a light bend to falling in or leaning in, he will pick up the wrong lead. To correct this, use more inside leg and inside indirect rein to move the horse wider on the curve, and ask again for the lead. The inside leg must not be the stronger cue or the wrong lead can happen again.

Natural Canter–Lengthened Canter–Natural Canter

HOW TO

The aids sequence to lengthen the stride at the canter is the same as you practiced to lengthen the walk and trot in the beginning exercises (see p. 111). As you practice this exercise on a curving line when your horse is bent to the inside, remember that your outside rein has to maintain contact to keep your horse

▲ *8.7 A–D* When lengthening at the canter, start on a straight line in natural canter (A). Use your seat with lots of weight in the saddle and light leg aids to drive your horse forward (B). As your horse starts to lengthen, he will further engage his hind legs under his body while lifting his forehand (C). The lengthened canter is still controlled with a connection from the leg to the hand, which encourages an actual lengthening without the horse's legs just moving more quickly (D).

straight and on the bit. It is also your "brake" rein. Your inside aids keep the horse bending while the outside rein slows the horse down, allowing him to engage the inside hind leg more (figs. 8.7 A–D).

Especially in the downward transition from lengthened canter to natural canter, a horse will break gait to the trot if you don't keep your driving aids active while using the outside rein to slow the stride. Again, you still encourage an uphill balance as with all other transitions, this one is just harder. You may have to use a short "check" with an upward action from your outside rein to get the horse to compact his body and shift his weight to the hind legs. Your rein is telling your horse, "More!" and "Now!"

COMMON CHALLENGES

☛ *Horse pulls on the reins:* If your horse is pulling down on the reins, he may not be ready for this transition. You can try using a quick upward check with your outside rein to remind him not to lose his balance forward as I explained earlier. If he has too much weight on the forehand from pulling on the reins, check to make sure that you did not create this situation from using too much rein aid; pulling on your reins; using your reins before your legs; or inconsistently using your seat and legs. Use a curved line during the transition to transfer weight onto the hind legs and help the slow down.

☛ *Horse "inverts" his topline:* When a horse struggles with upward transitions, he may be using his neck and front end to *pull himself* rather than rounding his back, and using his hind end to *push* into the faster gait. If you feel the upward transition starting from the forehand, take your horse on a curve, and ask him to move forward and *bend*. Raise your inside rein slightly and resist his above-the-bit actions, and spiral out by asking him to give to your inside leg (see p. 96). When he does, and your inside aids connect to your outside rein and leg, you have put him back in balance and on the bit. Forward motion engages the hind legs, brings the back up, and helps him give to the bit as you spiral out on the curving line. Once he has given to your inside rein and leg, and you are bending with the horse balanced between your legs and reins, simply start the transition again. Repeat until you get an improvement. It may take several tries. Improvement is training, so be patient.

TRAINING EXERCISE 13: Transitions at Markers

In order to get a transition at a specific moment, your horse has to be ready to respond when you ask him. Remember, you might need time to get him balanced, so incorporate that into your strategy when you want precision at a marker or letter (fig. 8.8).

Place four to six sets of markers approximately 3 feet apart on a curving line. The longer you make the curve, the more time you have to make transitions. You can practice picking up the walk, trot, or canter within the markers. After you master this, use two sets of markers and do the transition between them. You can then advance the exercise to only one set, and make the transition when your horse's shoulder or your leg is at the marker. This is the same strategy you use when doing a transition at a single cone in breed competitions or at a letter in dressage competitions (fig. 8.9).

Keep in mind these three letters—PPC. I use them to train myself to always: 1) prepare; 2) position; and 3) cue.

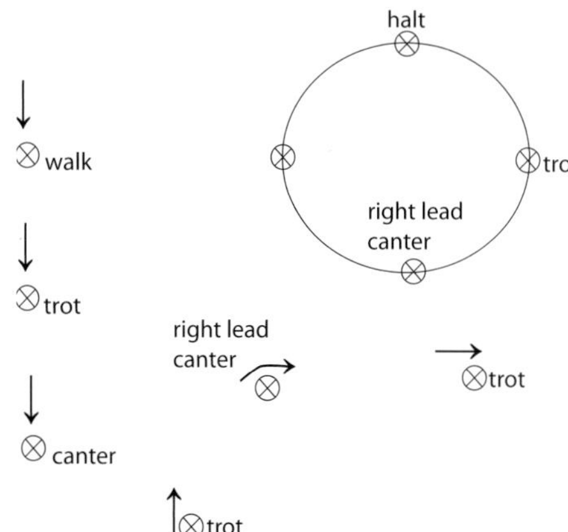

▲ *8.8* Examples of transitions at markers.

▲ *8.9* Your horse has to be in front of your leg (see p. 113) to perform transitions at certain points in the arena.

▲ *8.10* A poor downward transition onto the forehand can be caused by a rider's improper use of aids. Here I have thrown my shoulders back, braced my feet, and I am pulling on the reins—I am using all my aids at once rather than in the proper sequence.

1) *Prepare* with your eyes. The earlier you look ahead, the more time you have to think about what you want to accomplish and to review your aids.
2) *Position* your aids and get ready to cue. Don't position and cue at the same time. Position and wait, so your horse has time to recognize the position of your aids.
3) *Cue* your horse gradually with your sequence of aids.

COMMON CHALLENGES

☛ *Rider rushes the steps:* One of the biggest challenges of riding with precision is bunching together PPC all at the same moment. Having several sets of cones helps by training you *not to hurry.* Remember to take each step separately—*prepare—position—cue* (fig. 8.10).

☛ *Rider cues too late:* Cueing should be done at no later point than 10 feet before a marker so you can get the transition on time. Cue your horse and get a response. Most riders cue at the marker, so the transition always occurs afterward. Remember, when you cue, the horse has to have time to understand it, think of the appropriate action, and respond.

Jane Savoie on Collection

▲ *8.11* Jane Savoie on Menno, her Friesian.

Jane Savoie has been a competing member of the US Equestrian Team, as well as coach at three Olympics. She is a United States Dressage Federation Bronze, Silver, and Gold medalist, and winner of nine Horse of the Year awards and three National Freestyle Championships. She is also a popular clinician and speaker at equine events worldwide.

"Every horse is built with approx 60 percent of his weight on his forehand and 40 percent behind," Jane says. "This is because his body is built like a table, with the head and neck out on one end. The head and neck by itself can weigh as much as 250 pounds! So the horse has more weight on his front legs, by nature. With dressage training we systematically teach the horse to shift his center of gravity off the forehand and onto the hindquarters to be better equipped to carry himself, or collect. As he loads the hind legs, the forehand becomes lighter, freer, and more agile.

"One exercise that everyone can do is frequent transitions, skipping a gait. An example is: five strides canter, five strides walk, five strides canter, five strides walk. Your goal is not to have any trot strides in between, which you will have in the beginning. As you advance, you will feel a marked shift in the center of gravity toward the horse's hind legs. Or you can do five strides trot, halt, five strides trot, halt. As you're doing the downward transition, visualize the horse lowering his croup and sitting down like a dog. Do this several times and then just ride your trot. See if you feel how the balance has been shifted off the front end toward the hind end.

"People generally equate collection with dressage, and they think that it is just for dressage horses. But the truth is it doesn't matter what breed of horse it is or what his job is—whether reining or dressage or jumping. A horse that is collected is simply more athletic and can do his job better."

TRAINING EXERCISE 14: Short Sequence Transitions

Short sequence transitions can be done at any gait to increase weight to the hind legs; improve uphill balance; and compact, round, and stretch the horse's body. I often do transitions every five strides. You can practice this exercise with all of the transitions you have already learned (see pp. 102, 111, and 112). Your horse will tell you when he can move on—this is when he does your current transition easily. You may have to be patient when you attempt the exercise, as you have to supple the muscles and joints to get more accurate, quick, and responsive transitions.

Your horse should start to anticipate—this tells you that you can be lighter with your aids. I love anticipation, because it's telling me that the horse understands and is able to do whatever I'm asking more easily.

COMMON CHALLENGES

☛ *Horse becomes less responsive:* You may have drilled the exercise too much. You have to reward an improved or correct response, and when you get it, be done with the exercise for that day.

☛ *Horse gets anxious:* Your horse may get to a point where he gets a little worried (fig. 8.12). Just take more strides in between each transition so he can "slow down his mind" and respond. When you see he has relaxed and is giving you smooth responses again, you can return to transitions every five strides. As I've mentioned, your horse has to be straight to do transitions without struggling.

▶ *8.12* My horse is confused. Doing too many transitions in too short a period of time can cause a horse to get anxious, as indicated by his raised head, upright ears, worried eyes, and tense mouth. He is thinking too fast and doesn't want to go forward.

Thinking Slow!

Bobbi Steele, always told me you can't teach a horse anything unless he's "thinking slow." If he's getting wound up and he's anticipating in a way that he's worried and hurried, you're going way too fast. Go back to something simpler. Think about how you can approach the more advanced exercise in a different way to keep your horse positive.

"Thinking slow" means *not tiring out the horse*. At my first Women Luv Horses event outside Charlotte, North Carolina, Martha Josey arrived from Texas. She is a barrel racing legend and such a dynamic lady. I was so proud she was going to be an educator with me at the event. She was an inspiration for the women attending.

As we were setting up the day before, Martha was riding a beautiful palomino stallion in the arena. She was probably there at least a half-hour, and all she did was walk. I caught her leaving the arena and said, "Martha, that's a nice horse!" She replied, "This is my next hopeful—my next great barrel horse!" I told her I really admired how she was doing everything quietly with him. She said, "Yes! I'm trying to make him so that when I go to new places, he's 'thinking slow.'"

I was so impressed by this. When your horse goes into the ring and he's "thinking slow"—in addition to being behaved, well mannered, and well trained—he's going to run his fastest. It's the riders who don't have control of their horse and his mind who don't get the good times.

Martha told me that the palomino was a typical young horse—take him somewhere new and his mind went at 10,000 miles an hour, with his concentration distracted by everything and his actions hurried. Walking was just her way to get him "thinking slow" and feeling confident about his new surroundings—as well as trusting his rider.

Most people would go in and lope to get the horse to concentrate and submit. This would only end up getting him fatigued. That is not training! Simply making a horse tired does not help him. Martha, knowing this, was walking her horse, and that I really appreciated. Try it the next time you need to help your horse "think slow." It works!

TRAINING EXERCISE 15: Simple Lead Changes

To do a simple lead change, practice the trot–canter–trot transition in Training Exercise 5 (see p. 102), but concentrate on reducing the number of trot strides in each transition. By this time, your horse should be correctly bending in both directions, though he may still be weaker on one side than the other. This is okay as long as you are aware of it and take longer to prepare him to change leads on his "weaker" side. The weak side is usually the harder lead for him to take.

HOW TO

Start in a left lead canter to the left and transition down to trot. Once you have established the trot, bend your horse to the right and ask for an upward transition to right lead canter. At first, you may find yourself trotting for 25 strides in between canters. The number of strides it takes doesn't really matter. What is important is to establish your trot, bend, then canter off on the new lead in a straight line. The figure eight is perfect for practicing this exercise (see p. 109).

When the horse can do this effortlessly, reduce the number of trot strides between transitions. Ultimately, you want to establish two or three strides at the trot, and then pick up the new lead canter.

COMMON CHALLENGES

☛ *Horse takes fewer than two trot strides:* When your horse gets proficient at doing simple changes through the trot, he may take one or fewer strides at the trot, which means the horse is "ahead," and the rider is not controlling the simple lead change. The horse is doing the change on his own.

You must always be in control of your horse. If not, other problems will arise. When this happens, go back to five strides of trot—count out loud—and then canter. By slowing down you take more charge of controlling the horse's body position and speed in gait. Once you have control back, return to two to three strides at the trot to accomplish the perfect simple change of lead.

TRAINING EXERCISE 16: Yielding on a Straight Line

Now, if you've perfected yielding on a diagonal line, which you learned in chapter 7 (see p. 000), you can advance to yielding on a straight line (fig. 8.13). Both these exercises share the same rider aids sequence and horse-body alignment and balance. When working in an arena, this exercise is always practiced down the long side.

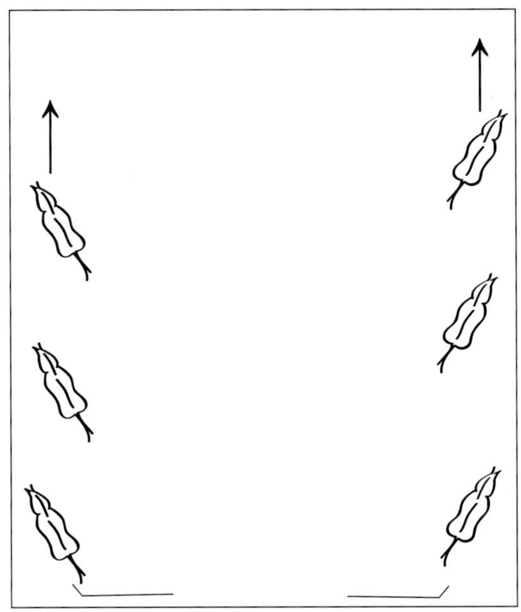

▲ *8.13* Yielding on a straight line.

▲ *8.14* When yielding on a straight line going to the right, your horse travels on four tracks, with his body straight and his head slightly flexed left.

HOW TO

Begin by walking to the right around the track—your right side (inside) faces the center of the arena. As you come out of a corner and begin to head down the long side, flex your horse's head slightly to the left—away from the direction you are yielding—just enough to see his eye (fig. 8.14).

With your left leg, ask him to yield his body to the right. The goal is to have your horse's shoulders remain on the rail, while his hips move inward onto a new track. His legs will travel on four independent tracks, and his body will be at approximately a 30-degree angle to the rail. Your right indirect rein has contact with the neck to keep his shoulder on the rail. When I teach riders this movement, they truly learn the importance of the right rein in controlling the shoulder, as well as use of their right leg to keep the horse's hind legs traveling with straight, even lateral steps.

COMMON CHALLENGES

☛ *Horse is crooked:* The most common challenge riders deal with is the crooked horse—that is, one whose hips or shoulders are not in a straight line. When you are not sure about the position of your horse's body, but recognize he is slowing down (most common) or speeding up (less common), have someone video you from the front. You will then know which aids you need to use to straighten him. Remember, forward motion is your first tool for straightening and for improving responses. When you add the correct aids, especially active outside rein and leg aids to achieve straightness, you will find improvement.

TRAINING EXERCISE 17: Yielding on a Curving Line

HOW TO

Ride a 70-foot (20-meter) circle to the left at the walk and pick up the trot (fig. 8.15). For one-quarter of the circle, keep your horse in a left bend as you follow the curve. At the next quarter, ask your horse to yield his body to the right. Your aids work in the same way as the yielding exercise on p. 136.

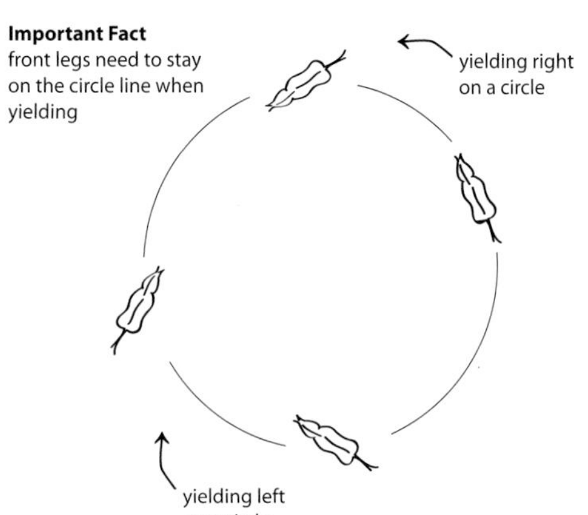

▲ *8.15* Yielding on a circle.

Your left leg has the same responsibility of moving the horse's body laterally to the right. Your right supporting rein and right leg aid straighten the horse's body alignment from being bent as he moves laterally. The horse's hips, which were slightly inward when maintaining the left bend, now move outward as his body alignment becomes straight in order to yield laterally. His body should be at an approximate 30-degree angle to the curved track. Maintain the straightness with the right rein and right leg, while keeping the head flexed to the left with a left open or indirect rein.

This is an excellent exercise for stretching and loosening up the hind legs. I love to use it to develop a balanced canter departure. When you are yielding to the right on a left circle, the left leg has to reach underneath the horse and swing sideways, which encourages the stretch and builds coordination of the hind limb. As your horse finishes the sideways movement, his weight and power is on the right hind leg, which is the first leg that pushes off into the left lead canter. Yielding during a transition from the walk or trot to the canter naturally puts the horse in a position to initiate the canter with power. Once you get your canter, reestablish the left bend, and ride on your curve or circle again.

COMMON CHALLENGES

☛ *Horse doesn't stay on the curving line:* When your circle gets bigger from the yielding and you are tracking left and yielding to the right, your supporting right indirect rein and leg are not being effective enough so the horse can move against them. Use a lighter left leg, and be more active with your right rein and leg aids to keep the horse's front legs on an inside track and his body yielding on the circle.

TRAINING EXERCISE 18: Shoulder-Fore

HOW TO

The shoulder-fore is practiced on the arena track next to the rail (figs. 8.16 A & B). Use a corner to help you get started. I like to do a 50-foot (15-meter) circle in the corner first to help me establish a correct bend to my horse's body before I go down the long side. The horse is angled away from the rail and moves on four tracks. His body, however, won't be as straight as it was when he was yielding on a straight line. This time, he keeps a light bend to his body (fig. 8.17 A).

When you track to the left, your horse is slightly bent to the left in the direction of travel. Your right rein brings the horse's shoulders off the rail and your left leg keeps his hips on the track. Your right leg keeps the horse's hips from swinging out, and the left rein maintains the flexion of the head to the left and keeps the horse on the bit as he moves laterally. The horse's front legs and hind legs should cross evenly on the four tracks (fig. 8.17 B).

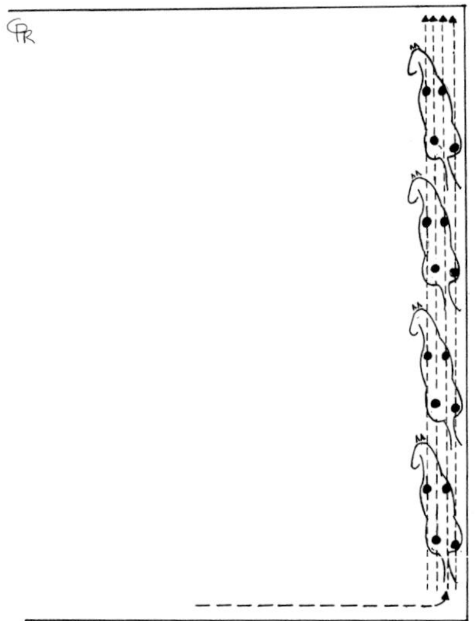

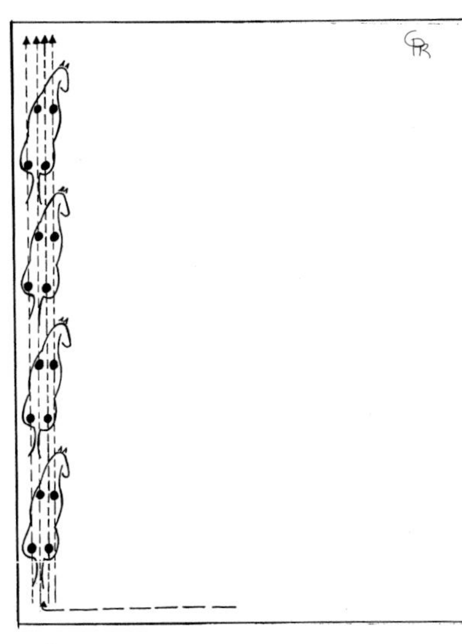

◀ *8.16 A & B* Shoulder-fore to the left (A) and to the right (B).

▶ *8.17 A & B* During the shoulder-fore exercise to the left, the horse continues to move on four tracks (A). His body has a slight bend to the left. He is balanced, moving laterally, and stepping well under himself (B).

COMMON CHALLENGES

☛ *Horse loses bend:* When this happens, encourage the bend with your left leg (when tracking left). Your left rein flexes his head in, and your right rein keeps him straight while bending (see p. 87) and prevents him from becoming crooked. Your right leg supports the bend by moving the horse's hips slightly to the inside.

☛ *Horse slows down:* Keep your driving aids active. Use your seat more aggressively and add more leg pressure for forward movement. Your left leg also moves the horse laterally when tracking left. If needed, use your voice or a crop to help.

TRAINING EXERCISE 19: Turn on the Haunches

After a horse has learned shoulder-fore, I move on to turn on the haunches—another lateral movement where the horse slightly bends his body in the direction of travel (figs. 8.18 A & B). This is the only exercise I offer where the Western version differs slightly from the dressage movement. In Western riding—where it is also called a "pivot"—the inside hind leg stays stationary. In dressage, the inside hind leg does *not* stay still on the ground, but moves in an up-and-down action in place.

There are three ways to practice, which I describe below. The first is on the ground with in-hand training, where you can see your horse's body position, the action of his legs, and how straightness in his body alignment allows him to turn tightly and laterally with his front legs. The second and third exercises are both done under saddle.

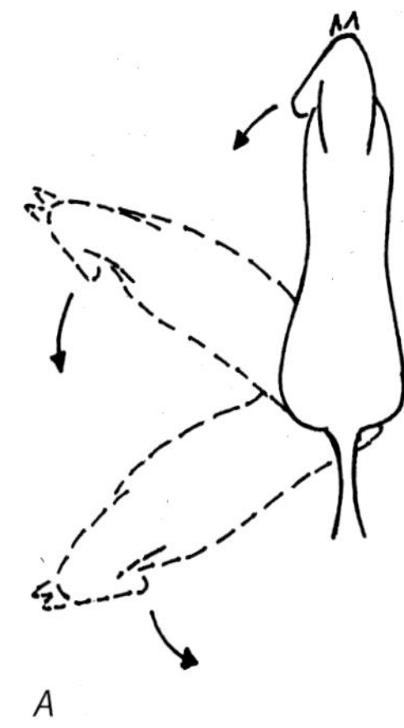

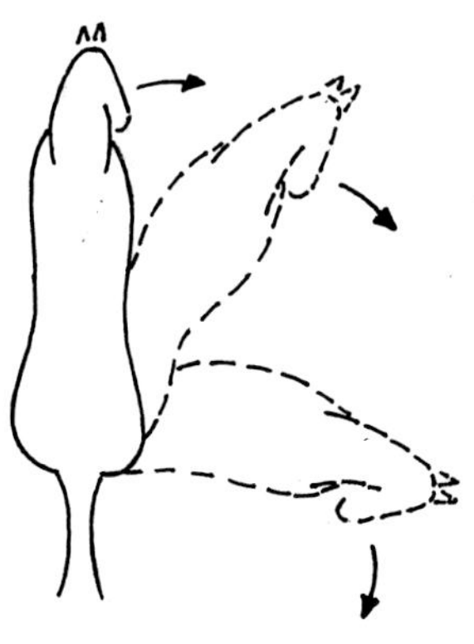

▲ *8.18 A & B* Turn on the haunches to the left (A) and to the right (B).

HOW-TO: ON THE GROUND

When I teach turn on the haunches on the ground, I want the horse to move away from pressure. On the ground, you cannot teach the bend; the horse has to be straight. I use one hand to hold the side of the halter to control the head and keep the horse from stepping forward (and certainly not backward). With the other hand, I make a fist and apply pressure on the side of the point of the shoulder. You are asking your horse's front legs to move sideways away from your pressure on the shoulder while keeping his body straight, so the hind legs will stay still. I then advance the movement and move my fist to where my leg aid would be under saddle and cue him from there. This more closely simulates a turn on the haunches under saddle.

HOW TO: UNDER SADDLE

When you begin this movement under saddle, you want your horse's body bent slightly in the direction of the turn (fig. 8.19). Your aid sequence is the same as bending (see p. 88). For a turn on the haunches to the left, use your left leg behind the girth to begin the bend and your left open rein to flex his head in slightly. Your right leg keeps the horse's hips from swinging out and your right indirect rein keeps his head from flexing too far in and his shoulder from bulging out. When teaching this exercise, move your right leg even further back to encourage the haunches to turn in the smallest diameter.

The first way I like to do a turn on the haunches under saddle is with my horse parallel to the rail. With the horse slightly bent, start by walking down the rail, then come to a straight, complete halt using the outside rein. A split second later, ask for your turn on the haunches. You want the horse to keep his bend and turn his front end around at the same time.

The second exercise is to go from a natural walk to a shortened stride, and then do the turn on the haunches through the shorter stride. You have to do it from the walk in dressage in order to keep the inside hind leg moving.

At the end, I like to walk out of the turn because, as with all movements, you don't want any backward steps. When you finish, use both legs together to move forward out of the turn and keep the horse's hind legs active and moving forward. Straighten your horse's body by using your diagonal leg and rein aids—your left leg pushes his hips out of the bend while your right rein straightens his head.

Start your turn on the haunches training by making a 90-degree turn. You can work your way up to 180 degrees, 270 degrees, and finally 360 degrees, which is a complete turn, once around.

▶ *8.19* During a turn on the haunches, your horse needs to have a slight bend to his body. His front legs move laterally.

COMMON CHALLENGES

☛ *Horse pivots on the wrong leg:* There are two reasons a horse pivots on the outside hind leg instead of the inside: 1) He has lost momentum through the turn; or 2) the forehand is ahead of the hindquarters, which encourages the hips to swing out, thus setting the wrong hind leg.

First, when there is a loss of momentum, start with a smaller turn, such as 45 degrees instead of 90 degrees. Make sure you walk out of the turn. Check you are not pulling with your rein aids, as this can slow your horse down. In a turn to the left, use your left open rein and right indirect rein both with a sideways action. Second, when the forehand moves ahead of the hindquarters, use your right indirect rein aid more

◀ *8.20* Incorrect: My horse is crooked and has little momentum as we begin a turn on the haunches.

actively to keep the shoulders in line with the hips, and your left leg aid to maintain balance through the horse's bend and energy through the turn.

☛ *Horse is crooked:* The key is to recognize whether your horse is moving away from your leg aids rather than leaning or pushing against them when you start and/or during the turn (fig. 8.20). When doing a turn to the left, your horse has to yield lightly to your right leg and rein aids while keeping the bend during the turn. Most of the time when a horse is struggling with the turn, it's because the rider has become too strong with a rein aid. The horse then loses momentum, which causes crookedness.

Advanced Training Exercises

A horse will let you know when he is ready to move on to advanced collection exercises. He tells you by consistently doing the beginning and intermediate exercises smoothly and willingly. Usually, when you move up from intermediate to advanced exercises, a horse doesn't get quite as frustrated as he did moving from the beginning to the intermediate level. Since he's more physically fit, he can accept your requests for quicker responses and more difficult maneuvers. When he's not ready, you'll be able to read the signs through his ears, mouth, and tail (see p. 8).

Don't ever forget to give your horse time off. Don't just drill him in the ring. Go trail riding. Keep the lessons and the routine interesting. Remember, treat him like *you* want to be treated. This is what I'm known for with my performance horses in the show ring: They go in and they look happy. *Why* they're happy is what this book is all about.

The Half-Halt

The half-halt is used to balance and rebalance your horse. It is very effective when the horse goes on his forehand, gets a little "heavy," or fails to engage his hind-

◀ *9.1* As I close my right hand into a fist and drive with my seat and legs, you can clearly see the horse's energy translate *upward* rather than just *forward.*

quarters. It's a great tool as long as you know how to ride one correctly and only use it in moderation.

HOW TO

To perform a half-halt, close your fingers—making a fist—on your outside rein. The time it takes you to make a fist and execute the half-halt should be the same time it takes you to inhale. During this two or three seconds, continue to drive your horse forward with your seat and legs into the gradual closing of your fingers to a fist. This makes the horse think, "I'm going forward but in a compact frame." The energy you create to go forward then goes *vertical* rather than *horizontal* (fig. 9.1).

The properly executed half-halt produces somewhat the same result as when an ocean wave hits a jetty. The wave comes in with a lot of strength and speed, hits the jetty, and the water goes up instead of straight onto the land. What the jetty causes the water to do is what your hand—and your half-halt—does to your horse. All that energy produced from his hind end, instead of going straight out his front end and "vanishing" because the horse is long and flat, goes "up" into your outside hand. You are rebalancing your horse. Yes, you keep your horse from getting long, flat, and on the forehand, but at the same time, you also reenergize him. The half-halt gets the horse light in the forehand.

Some people think the half-halt is a quick jerk on the reins, which it's not. The two main problems I see are: 1) riders who pull back on their reins; and 2) those who don't drive the horse forward before the hand closes and forms a fist, which totally defeats the purpose. The half-halt should only be used by an advanced rider on an advanced horse. If you have not mastered the beginning and intermediate exercises in the previous two chapters, please do not attempt it. Used correctly, the half-halt is an effective tool to make sure your horse is balanced before you ask for a change of gait, speed, or direction.

TRAINING EXERCISE 20: Advanced Canter Transitions

Advanced transitions help to connect the horse even more from back to front, from the leg to the rein, and they promote an uphill frame and balance. A horse must be relaxed and straight, have impulsion, and have enough strength to be able to be connected. Canter transitions are the most difficult because they involve the greatest difference in speed, and the horse must be more rounded in order to accomplish the task. You will use the following transitions in this exercise:

- Shortened trot–canter–shortened trot

- Walk–canter–walk
- Natural canter–collected canter–natural canter
- Canter–halt–canter

Shortened Trot–Canter–Shortened Trot

The intermediate horse should be able to immediately pick up the canter from a natural trot before moving to this advanced exercise. Any time you take the horse's natural length of stride and shorten it, you make tasks more difficult because he has to compress his body and collect. He has to be further engaged to get more energy in order to go slower in an uphill balance. So when you begin this shortened trot to canter transition, your horse may struggle again.

The small circle within a large circle Training Figure (see p. 111) is excellent for practicing shortened trot–canter–shortened trot transitions. The small circle helps you prepare, as well as helps the horse concentrate and puts him into a more compacted balance so he can take the canter from a slower speed and then return to the shortened trot more easily.

HOW TO

To help the horse with this more advanced transition, begin by riding a 70-foot (20-meter) circle at a natural trot. Transition to a shortened trot by asking your horse to slow down and shorten his stride on a smaller circle. As with any downward transition, use your seat and leg aids to maintain forward motion while using your rein aids to slow the horse, asking him to round his back, shorten his stride and "collect" (see p. 102). Three-quarters of the way around the smaller circle, ask for the canter depart. If your horse doesn't pick up the canter in the last quarter, stop and start over. Once you establish the canter, ride the larger 70-foot (20-meter) circle. When you are ready for the downward transition to the shortened trot, return to the small circle.

COMMON CHALLENGES

- *Horse "pulls himself" into the canter:* When this happens, the horse struggles to engage his hindquarters and round his back because he is using his head and neck to pull himself into the upward transition. Don't trot quite so slowly at first. When you add a little more speed, your horse will have the extra forward motion to propel himself into the canter. Then, when he is comfortable with the in-between pace, reintroduce the slower, shortened trot and try again.

- *Horse inverts and/or falls on the forehand in the downward transition:* Both of these problems will make the transition abrupt rather than smooth and are usually the

result of a rider using her hands too quickly, or the horse not engaging his hind end to be in an uphill balance. Allowing a horse to slow down through the natural trot first and then slowing to the shortened stride is preferable to the horse going on the forehand or inverting. Allow him to gradually slow down with a canter–natural trot–shortened trot transition on the larger circle rather than letting him lose his rounded frame and uphill balance. As you get more proficient, reduce the length of time it takes you to get to the shortened trot.

Walk–Canter–Walk

Before you attempt the walk–canter–walk transition, your horse should be capable of three speeds at the walk—natural, lengthened, and shortened. He should also do a natural canter, lengthened canter, and be starting to show strides of shortened canter. You need to be able to shorten your horse's stride at the walk while keeping his body rounded and in an uphill balance.

HOW TO

When I ask a horse to do the walk–canter transition, I first control his natural speed at the walk. Then, I shorten the stride and create a light bend while keeping the energy going with my driving aids, and ask for the canter depart.

My favorite exercise for this upward transition is to ride a 35-foot (10-meter) circle at the walk because the circle naturally puts the rider in a position to easily collect the horse. Ask for the canter depart between three-quarters of the way around and the completion of the circle.

The downward canter–walk transition is all about the horse's uphill balance (figs. 9.2 A–C). Ask the horse to slow down at the three-quarter mark of the circle, or in the case of an already advanced horse, when the circle is nearly completed. When I begin teaching this transition, I let the horse trot on his way down, rather than asking for a perfect canter to walk. This is

◀ *9.2 A–C* In any transition exercise, always remember PPC: *prepare, position,* and *cue*. Prepare your horse for the canter–walk transition by looking ahead to where you want the walk (A). Once you have *prepared*, then *position* your aids, and *cue* your horse (B). The walk is easily accomplished (C).

the perfect transition to practice a half-halt: shorten your horse's canter stride and rebalance him before asking for the walk (see p. 145).

COMMON CHALLENGES

☛ *Horse fails to collect:* Your goal is to eliminate any trot steps, which were initially used to slow down to the walk while maintaining uphill balance. As you ask your horse to slow down, add more leg pressure to keep his hind end engaged and use your outside "brake" rein with quick, sharp checks to rebalance, collect and then slow down to the walk (fig. 9.3). The timing is essential for a correct response. You can use cones to help you visualize, then *prepare* and *position* your aids, and *cue* the horse to get the walk sooner. Review—and perfect—the lengthened trot to walk transition (see p. 111).

▲ *9.3* Poor balance at the canter caused by my riding with no leg contact and no rein contact. Should I pick up the reins, the horse could easily run through my hands because he has so much weight on his front end.

Natural Canter–Shortened Canter–Natural Canter

HOW TO

When your horse is performing a natural canter stride and you want him to slow down and shorten it, he has to engage his hindquarters more. Begin cantering a curving line. As you start your aid sequence, sit with more weight on your inside seat bone. This helps the horse's inside hind leg engage further underneath him. You may want to use a half-halt to prepare your horse for the shortened stride (see p. 145). Your leg aids have to be active as you ask for the transition. Your inside aids continue to bend your horse while the outside direct rein asks your horse to compact his body and slow down. Training on a circle, which I discuss in the next Training Figure (the half-volte), is a great exercise. Try to ride a half-circle at natural canter; half circle at shortened canter; half-circle at natural canter; and half-circle at shortened canter, in sequence.

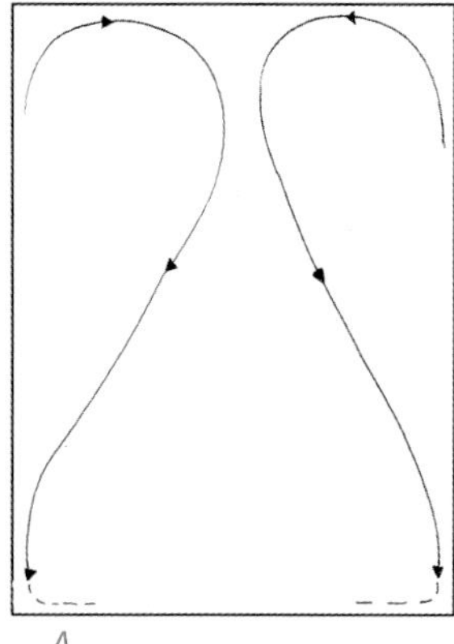
A

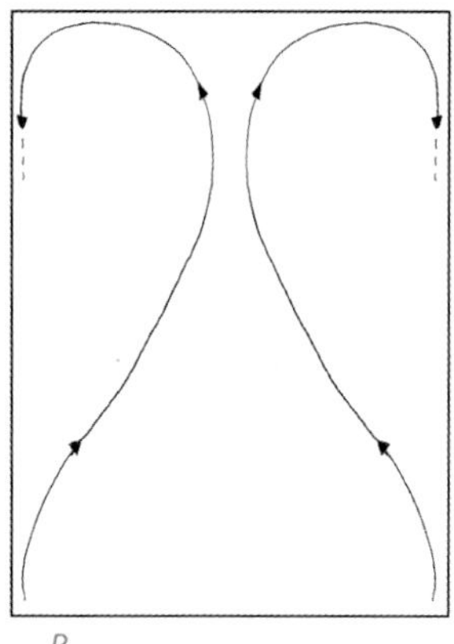
B

Training Figure: *Half-Volte (Half-Circle)*

Volte is the French world for circle, which may make this figure sound difficult, but it is not. The *half-volte* is an excellent way to change direction or practice transitions on a half-circle and straight line. Asking for the shortened stride at the beginning of the half-circle is a natural way to help your horse succeed with the downward transition.

In natural canter, ride down the long side of the arena, turn at the end, and in shortened canter start a half-circle that touches the centerline. As you complete the half-circle, straighten your horse, and in natural canter ride a diagonal line back to the long side where you started. When completed, do a simple change of lead through the trot or walk to go in the opposite direction and repeat the exercise (fig. 9.4 A).

This figure can be ridden in reverse—the *inverted half-volte*—by starting with a diagonal line toward the center (fig. 9.4 B). When you reach the centerline, far end turn back toward the long side, riding a half-circle followed by a straight line down the long side to complete the figure. Don't cut corners or rush the figure—if your half-circles are too small and not uniformly round, your straight line will be crooked. (For additional Training Figures, see the sidebar on p. 94).

◀ *9.4 A & B* A half-volte (A) and an inverted half-volte (B).

COMMON CHALLENGES

☛ *Horse doesn't shorten his stride:* Analyze your horse's body alignment. As you perfect his balance, you will get an improved response, and a more willing one. My mentor always told me: "React to your horse's reactions." Is your horse going too fast? Too slow? Leaning left? Turning right? If he's slowing down too much and falling on his forehand, add more leg. If he's losing his bend through the curve, add more inside leg or inside open rein. If he is cantering too fast, use less leg but don't take your leg off the horse's side. Pay attention to the horse's natural reactions as he responds to your cues.

Halt–Canter–Halt

When practicing the canter–halt transition, it's very easy to see the difference between a horse that is doing the maneuver correctly and one that's not. A horse performing this downward transition well has an uphill balance and will make a smooth stop. Incorrectly, he'll be on the forehand with a jarring stop.

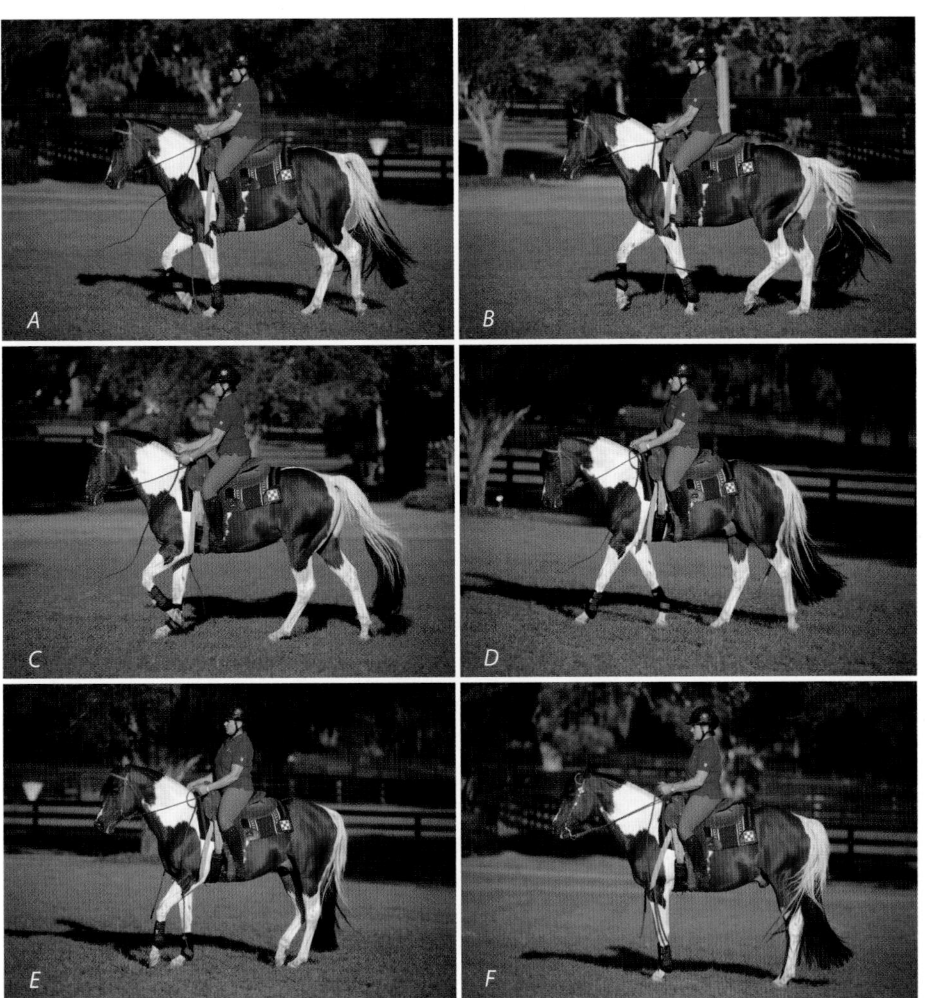

◀ *9.5 A–F* As you advance, you can combine transition exercises. Here I practice Walk–Canter and Canter–Halt to add variety to my training. You must bend your horse's body and shorten the walk before the transition to the canter (A). Your horse should stay relaxed through the upward transition (B). Here you see a desirable, uphill balance at the collected canter (C). Continue to canter for several strides while you prepare your horse for the downward transition to the halt. Transition smoothly and in balance, even if you get a few trot steps in between (D). As your horse's transitions improve, you will have fewer trot or walk steps from canter to halt (E). A horse that does this canter–halt transition correctly should stop smoothly, straight, and balanced (F).

HOW TO

This exercise is done in three stages: First, canter a 70-foot (20-meter) circle, halt, and return to the canter (figs. 9.5 A–F). To keep your horse round and in front of your leg, the time you spend at the halt must be minimal—not more than a few seconds. Next, advance to a half-circle: Pick up the canter between one set of markers, canter a half-circle, halt, and canter off again. Finally, advance to performing a halt–canter–halt at each quarter of the circle. By the time you reach this stage, your horse will be cantering four to six strides between each transition.

To take the halt–canter–halt exercises to an even more advanced level, change from working on a curving line to working on a straight line. These are the fundamentals for flying lead changes: You control the horse's body position for a bend on one lead, halt, change the bend for the new lead, and canter on the new lead (see more about flying changes on p. 163). It's an excellent exercise to strengthen and condition the longitudinal muscles, create suppleness and flexibility of the spine, and build the first real stages of getting your horse maximally collected.

COMMON CHALLENGES

☛ *Horse struggles to pick up the canter:* To perfect the upward halt–canter transition, the horse must not wiggle side to side (see p. 95) or take any walk or trot steps. Many riders mistakenly have been taught that pushing their horse's hip to the inside helps their horse pick up the correct lead. You are actually making him crooked and thus making it harder for him to pick up the canter. When the hip is excessively inward, the shoulders go outward and the head, inward. This loss of straightness causes the horse to have a delayed response, which takes away the power he needs to perform the transition. You will see the rider ask, and the horse will wait, wait, wait, struggle, and then canter off.

A horse that remains crooked as he canters can't go forward easily. Mentally, he won't be happy, and physically, it causes a lot of wear and tear on his body. For the horse to have maximum "pushing" power from the hind end, he has to be in straight alignment. When he is lightly bent in the direction of the lead and totally in balance, he can just float off into that canter.

TRAINING EXERCISE 21: Counter-Canter

This important training exercise teaches the horse to be balanced with an "off-balance" maneuver. Counter-cantering is simply cantering on the wrong lead. For example, when you are going to the left, the right lead would be in counter-canter, and vice versa. When you are on the counter-canter lead, the horse must stay balanced and maintain a counter bend of the body, which is in the direction of the lead.

Training Figure: *Loop on Both Long Sides*

I love to introduce the counter-canter with this loop Training Figure (fig. 9.6). It is the easiest way to keep the bend, improve balance, and stay on the counter-canter lead without the horse falling in and changing leads.

Tracking left at the canter, in the left corner coming out of the short side of the ring, make a left curving line toward "X" (the center of the ring on the centerline and middle of the width of the ring). Before you get there, straighten your horse and maintain a slight bend to the left as "X" becomes the middle of a curve to the right. Finish the right curve after "X," straighten and keep the slight bend left, and turn left in the corner to continue on a left track. You can do the figure again on the other long side of the ring going in the same direction. (See the sidebar on p. 94 for more Training Figures.)

You can advance from the loop to a large circle 140-feet (40 meters) in diameter, then to a serpentine, maintaining the same lead throughout its loops. When your horse is supple and balanced and can keep the bend easily, you can try a 70-foot (20-meter) circle.

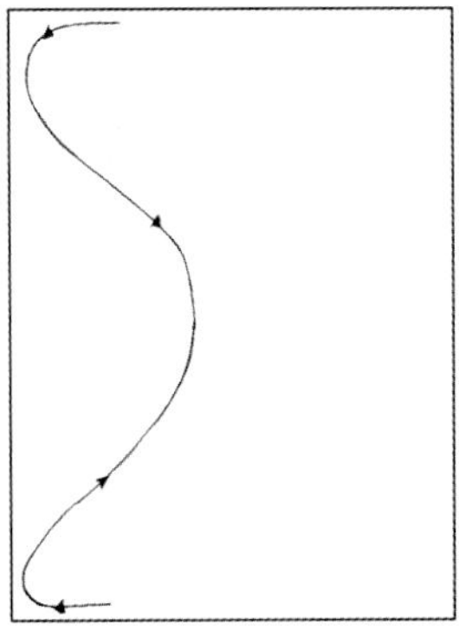

▲ *9.6* A loop.

COMMON CHALLENGES

☛ *Horse breaks gait:* When the horse breaks to the trot, your circle or the curved lines of your Training Figure are too small, or the horse is falling in. Use a larger circle or curve. Keep the horse bent to the right for a right-lead counter-canter and left for a left counter-canter. He will not trot when you are keeping him correctly straight and balanced.

☛ *Horse gets quick and/or stiff:* When your horse quickens his stride, becomes stiff, and resists the counter-canter, he is not in a correct balance. Go back to the trot and practice the loop or half-circle figures with a counter bend at the trot—or walk if you have real difficulties. Doing so will give you a tool for the counter-canter, and also slow the horse's mind so he can start to understand what you want.

TRAINING EXERCISE 22: Shoulder-In

The shoulder-in is a progression from the shoulder-fore (see p. 139). It requires more bend, and when you're tracking to the left, the horse's body is bent to the left (figs. 9.7 A & B). The horse moves on three tracks instead of four and his legs are as follows: the right hind is on the track closest to the rail; the left hind and right front are on the same track; and the left front is on a third track closer to the center of the arena (fig. 9.8).

HOW TO

As I progress from shoulder-fore to shoulder-in, I use a smaller circle of 35-feet (10-meters) in diameter to start the exercise, as a smaller circle requires more bend. The aids sequence is the same as for shoulder-fore: on a left track, bend your horse slightly to the left; your right rein brings his shoulders off the rail; your left

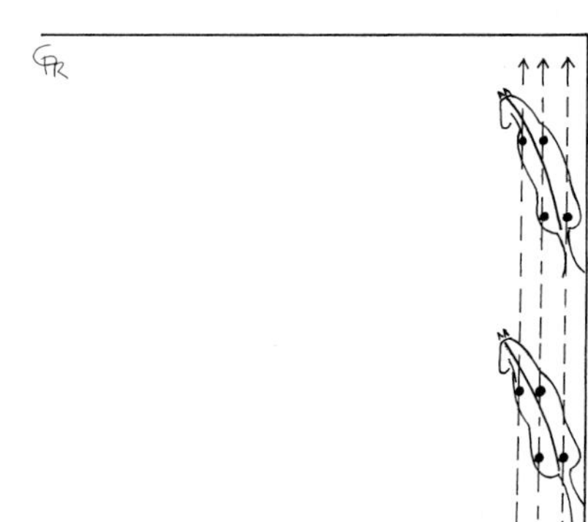

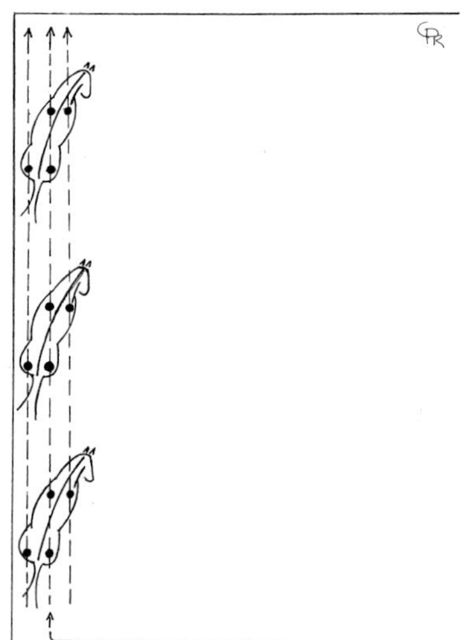

▲ *9.7 A & B* Shoulder-in to the left (A) and to the right (B).

▲ *9.8* When practicing shoulder-in, your horse moves on three tracks with more bend to his body than in the easier shoulder-fore exercise (see p. 139).

leg keeps his hips on the track; your right leg keeps his hips from swinging out, and your left rein flexes his head to the left. Your left rein is the most passive aid. The horse must respond more from the left leg to the right rein to stay straight while bending.

Compared to the shoulder-fore, in the shoulder-in the horse has to be more forward with additional energy, flexing the hind leg joints and engaging the hind legs. He must also round his spine more, get lighter in the front legs, and take more weight onto his hindquarters to achieve it, particularly with the inside hind leg. This exercise improves his fitness, balance, and ability to collect.

COMMON CHALLENGES

☛ *Horse does not bend:* Move your left leg slightly back. If you get no reaction, change the way you apply your left leg: Start by vibrating your foot and then tap with your leg, and if you still don't get a response, bump harder with the leg. Do not hesitate to use spurs when needed but *do not* kick your horse with them. Also, try riding a circle or two before resuming the shoulder-in exercise. Sometimes this is all it takes for the horse to bend.

☛ *Horse leaves the rail:* When your horse tries to leave the rail instead of bending and achieving shoulder-in when tracking left, he could be ignoring your left leg. Try the same progression of left leg aid as described in the previous challenge—vibrate your foot, tap with your leg, bump harder, and add a spur. Also, make a fist with your outside hand and hold tension on the rein to keep the horse's right shoulder on the rail.

☛ *Horse swings his hips outward:* If instead of bending to the left when tracking left, the horse pushes his hips against your right leg, move your right leg back to "hold" the horse's hips in place. You might have to hold your leg at that spot until the horse understands that he needs to respect the pressure of the right leg. More often than not, when the horse's hips swing outward, it is because the rider is pulling back with the left rein. This bends the neck too far inward, which throws the hips out.

TRAINING EXERCISE 23: Haunches-In

Haunches-in is an exercise where the horse's hind end is brought inward off the track (figs. 9.9 A & B). It is similar in one respect to shoulder-in, in that the horse's body position, alignment, roundness of the spine, and arc of the body for the movement stay the same. The horse is bent in the direction he is traveling, and his legs move on three tracks. We also sometimes describe this exercise as the horse moving along the rail with his "head to the wall."

HOW TO

To train haunches-in to the left, the horse must bend to the left while his hips come off the rail and the shoulders stay on the rail. Start by tracking to the left, with your horse bending left on a straight line. Bring the haunches in with your right leg while maintaining the bend with your left leg. Your left indirect rein holds the shoulders on the rail, although you might have to use an open rein if your horse tries to avoid the movement by moving his forehand toward the rail. The right indirect rein supports the bend so that the head doesn't go too far left and the shoulders don't go right (figs. 9.10. A & B).

To go from haunches-in to a straight line, use your left leg to straighten the hips, and your right indirect rein to straighten the head, neck, and shoulders to line up with the hips. On the long side of the ring,

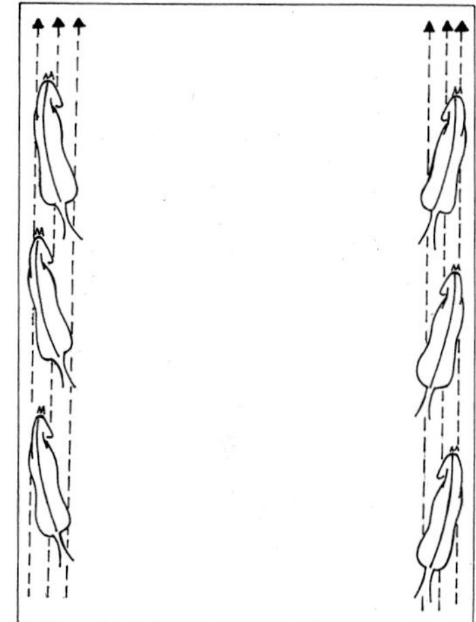

A

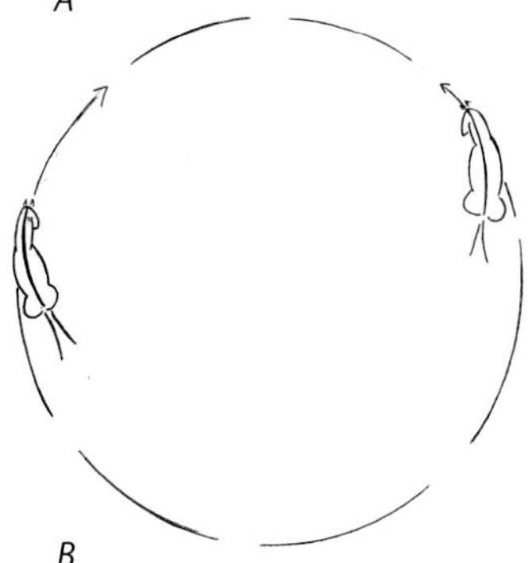

B

▶ *9.9 A & B* Haunches-in on straight (A) and curved (B) lines.

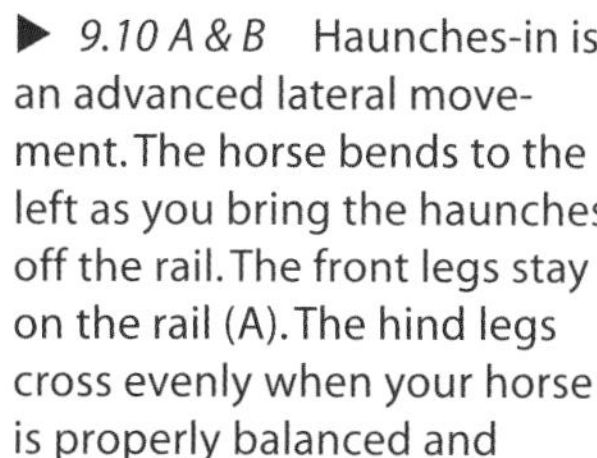

▶ *9.10 A & B* Haunches-in is an advanced lateral movement. The horse bends to the left as you bring the haunches off the rail. The front legs stay on the rail (A). The hind legs cross evenly when your horse is properly balanced and straight (B).

start by asking your horse for a few strides of haunches-in at a time, and gradually extend the number of strides as your horse progresses.

COMMON CHALLENGES

☛ *Horse's hips come too far forward:* The horse has too much angle in relation to the rail. Usually, this is caused by a rider who uses too much outside leg to move the horse's hips inward. The horse cannot stay forward when moving at too great of an angle (45 degrees or more). He will start slowing down and stop engaging, and resist by bringing his head above the bit. Send the horse forward and straight with your seat and inside leg until the hips move back closer to the correct angle, then resume the movement. This time, do not move your outside leg too far back.

☛ *Horse's shoulder falls out toward the rail:* When the horse's forehand does not stay next to the rail, it usually creates a loss of bend. Use an indirect outside rein close to the neck while your outside leg presses lightly at the girth. Both outside aids keep the horse straight while executing the movement.

☛ *Horse does not move his hips inward:* He could be speeding up and pulling on the reins. Always regulate speed first by using the outside rein to control it. If you still have difficulty, transition to a slower gait or stop him. He must understand that when you ask the hips to move, it is not a signal to speed up.

Cyril Pittion-Rossillon on Yielding

A native of France, Cyril Pittion-Rossillon earned the prestigious Riding Master Degree from the French National Equestrian School, where he was instructed by members of the French Olympic Team. An accomplished competitor in jumping, dressage, and three-day eventing, he trained other young professionals at the largest equestrian center in Paris, the Brimborion Equestrian Center. Upon moving to the United States in 1989, Pittion-Rossillon continued competing in AQHA and USEF events. Today, he co-directs and conducts Palm Partnership Equestrian Schools, and is cofounder and Managing Director of Alliance Saddlery.

"Yielding is one of the more difficult concepts for a horse and rider to master," he says. "More often than not, it takes a while for the horse to understand this exercise, and you go through some confusion, resistance, and many ups and downs before the horse finally learns. Then it becomes a movement that is very important to your training, and because you have gone through the ups and downs, you end up stronger on the other side.

"I had an Appendix Quarter Horse mare that was brought to me several years ago. She was ultra-sensitive. She had been pushed and rushed, and was probably one of the most difficult, if not *the* most difficult horse I have ever had to ride. She would literally 'run' at the trot and at the canter. She would just grab the bit and run. Yielding really helped me get her to concentrate, focus, calm down, and pay attention to my aids. When I was able to ask her to move away from my aids and she would do so softly, she was basically starting to tell me, 'Okay Cyril, I'm going to start responding to you and I'm going to start complying. I'm going to start trusting you.' That's when we started clicking.

"When the horse starts yielding really well and it's almost like second nature to him, you have reached a different level in your rapport."

▲ *9.11* My husband, Cyril Pittion-Rossillon.

TRAINING EXERCISE 24: Haunches-Out

Haunches-out is the first lateral exercise I've offered in this book where the horse is bent in the opposite direction of travel—that is, in the direction of lateral movement—which makes it a more difficult maneuver (figs. 9.12 A & B). It is a mirror image of haunches-in (see p. 155). For example, in haunches-out to the left, the horse is bent in a left arc while tracking right. Do not attempt haunches-out if your horse does not already bend well on three different sized circles—70, 50, and 35 feet in diameter in both directions.

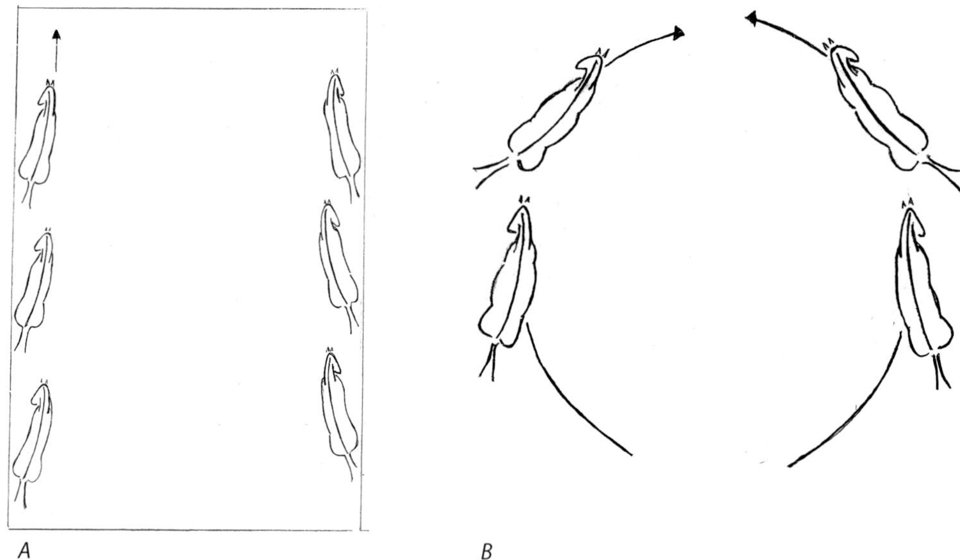

▲ *9.12 A & B* Haunches-out on straight (A) and curved (B) lines.

HOW TO

When you're tracking left with your horse bent to the left, go straight first. Then create a right bend with your right leg. Keep your horse's hips on the rail by using your left leg aid a little farther back to bend around the right leg aid. Move the forehand off the track using a right indirect rein to flex the head while supporting with the left rein. Keep a slight angle to the rail of approximately 30 degrees (figs. 9.13 A & B).

Start practicing this exercise on a straight line with the help of the rail. When you master it, ride it on a circle. Haunches-out is a more advanced exercise than haunches-in, but it brings the exact same benefits. Both are traditionally known as preparatory exercises for the half-pass (see p. 160).

▲ *9.13 A & B* In haunches-out, the horse is on an approximately *30*-degree angle to the rail and bent in the direction of lateral movement (A). Here you can see the hind legs moving laterally (B). Both these examples show the horse's forehand too far off the track—too far to the left—so the movement appears to be on four tracks when it should be on three, as with shoulder-in. I need to apply more left indirect rein to move the horse's shoulders to the right without losing the bend.

COMMON CHALLENGES

☛ *Horse does not bend/leans against your leg:* When tracking left, you can move your right leg a little farther back and see if your horse starts bending, or change the way you apply it: vibrate, tap, or bump more firmly. A small spur can be a very effective tool in encouraging the horse to bend his rib cage. When he still does not bend, it means he is not ready for the movement. Go back to practicing bending on a 35-foot (10-meter) circle and perfecting shoulder-in (see p. 153).

☛ *Horse moves away from the rail:* When you ask the horse to bend and he leaves the rail, close your fingers on your right rein (when tracking left) to tell him to keep his forehand only slightly off the track by the rail and not to move more inward.

TRAINING EXERCISE 25: Half-Pass

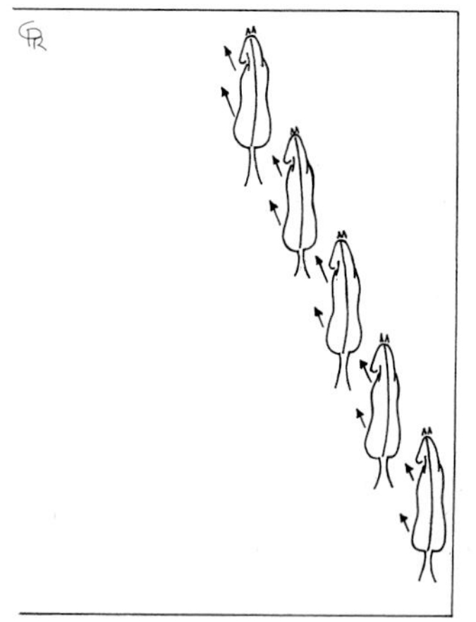

A

B

▲ *9.14 A & B* Half-pass to the left (A) and to the right (B).

The half-pass is an exercise where the horse moves laterally on a diagonal line while bending in the direction of travel (figs. 9.14 A & B). His body stays parallel to the rail while the forehand is positioned slightly ahead of the hind end. For example, for a half-pass to the left, the horse moves sideways and forward to the left while maintaining a left bend. To do this maneuver, the horse has to be already responsive to a light leg action, whether to go forward or move the hips away from pressure. He must bend easily in both directions on a 35-foot (10-meter) circle, in all three gaits. He should also be comfortable in an uphill balanced frame and experienced with all the lateral movements leading up to the half-pass—a movement that requires the horse to bend his body while crossing his legs with a great degree of extension (figs. 9.15 A & B).

HOW TO

For a half-pass to the right, walk a straight line and ask your horse to bend to the right. Your right leg applies pressure just behind the girth to bend your horse; your right open rein flexes his head slightly to the right. Your left leg is further back than your right to move the horse's hips to the right as he bends his body around your right leg. Your left indirect rein on the horse's neck keeps him straight while bending. Once he is bending to the right on a straight line, change to a diagonal line and ask for haunches-in. Your left indirect rein and left leg actively move the horse's forehand to the right. Your right leg and rein aids maintain the bend.

If you have done your homework and mastered all the earlier lateral movements—in particular, haunches-in and -out—the half-pass should be fairly easy for you and your horse. It's really a beautiful movement, and one that helps the horse achieve a greater degree of balance and collection. When you have mastered the half-pass, you are well on your way to performing the most advanced movements, such as flying lead changes and canter pirouettes. The half-pass can be ridden in all three gaits.

COMMON CHALLENGES

☛ *Horse leads with the hips:* A horse can start moving crookedly when a rider uses too much leg. For example, in a half-pass to the left, too much left leg for bend causes the horse to lose his straightness. Another reason the horse may lead with his hips has to do with the positioning of the forehand. When you let the horse's shoulder fall out, the hips will move in: so going to the left, if the right shoulder falls out to the right, the hips will compensate by moving to the left. To correct

▲ *9.15 A & B* My horse is exhibiting a correct and beautifully balanced half-pass (A). His forehand is positioned slightly ahead of his hind end, and his hind legs step well under his body to cross (B).

this, use a left open rein and bring the right indirect rein against the neck while asking the horse to stay sideways and forward.

☛ *Horse leads too much with the forehand:* When the horse's forehand is too far ahead of his hips, his body is no longer parallel to the rail. Usually the horse is leaning against your bending rein and basically trying to "break" the bend. Going to the left, make sure you are not pulling back on your left rein as you ask the horse to flex his head. Move your left leg back a little bit and slightly raise your left indirect rein, applying it against the horse's neck without crossing over the withers or crest. Keep contact with your right rein to regulate the bend of the neck. As soon as the horse stops leaning, drop your left hand down and reward your horse.

My Royal Lark

My Royal Lark was a beautiful stallion by Rugged Lark. By the time he was 10 years young, he had followed all of the training exercises in this book in arenas, pastures, on trails, and at horse shows. In competition, he had done hunter on the flat and over fences, trail, and Western riding. I wanted to make him a true all-around athlete and accomplish success in dressage. I had him doing flying lead changes. He could do five- and four-tempi changes (every fifth and fourth stride), but his three-tempis were always inconsistent.

▲ *9.16* My Royal Lark loved a variety of disciplines. Correct collection allowed him to perform at his best no matter what he was doing.

So, I went to have an evaluation and lesson with Jane Savoie, one of my dearest friends and an international competitor and wonderful educator in dressage (see sidebar on p. 133). I went through all the moves with my horse, and she said, "Your horse is doing Fourth Level movements, but you haven't developed his body enough to be in the collected frame that he needs at this level. You're going to need another year to two years to get more of a collected physique. You should start working your horse at Second Level, and he will really shine."

For a whole year I just did Second Level because I wanted to qualify for Regionals, which he did easily and I got great scores. By the end of the year, I had perfected a simple change of lead—canter–walk–canter. There were no trot steps, my horse didn't wiggle or push his hips to the inside, or get crooked in any way during the transitions. It was canter to walk, walk two strides keeping the balance and the straightness, right into a powerful, beautiful canter. Guess what? When I went back to my three-tempi lead changes, they were right there. We never made another mistake.

When I reviewed the simpler change of lead through walk, I perfected my own skills, the timing of my aids, and the control of my horse's balance. I got my horse more collected, in more of an uphill balance. The moral of this story is, when you want to advance a maneuver but your ride is inconsistent, always go back to basics. Then, when you go back to the harder movements, they will be right there, waiting for you.

TRAINING EXERCISE 26: Flying Lead Changes

Although there are several different training exercises for flying lead changes, all of the previous exercises are the fundamentals that lead to them. For me, the flying lead change is the last foundation in the basics. When your horse completes all of the tasks in this book, you can move on in any discipline and advance your horse to the specialization that is required. I teach the flying lead change in four stages:

1) Change leads with a natural length of stride, and let the horse do it on his own.
2) Change leads in a figure eight.
3) Change leads from yielding.
4) Change leads from counter-canter to correct lead; then advance to changing from correct lead to counter lead.

Change Leads with a Natural Length of Stride

HOW TO

Use the Training Figure changing direction from a diagonal line to practice this exercise (see p. 95). On a left track, ride a forward, balanced left-lead canter with your horse bent to the left (fig. 9.17 A). As you turn the corner leaving the short side and begin to cross the diagonal, straighten your horse as you did in the simple lead change exercise (see p. 136) and flex his head in the new direction—to the right (fig. 9.17 B). As you begin your curving line at the far end of the diagonal, apply your left leg aid to ask for the right lead canter, and the horse should move his hips to complete his right bend (fig. 9.17 C). If you don't get the lead change at this moment, use a crop and tap just behind your leg.

▶ *9.17 A–C* I begin across the diagonal on the left lead, my horse slightly bent to the left (A). As I approach the end of the diagonal line, I've flexed his head slightly to the right and he moves his hips in preparation for the change (B). He completes the change to the right lead and we can continue on a curving line to the right (C).

COMMON CHALLENGES

☛ *Horse changes lead in front but not behind:* This happens when the shoulder falls inward and the hips swing out. The horse cannot make the change with the hind leg if he is not straight on the diagonal line. Check your balance and position, and your horse's body position. He has to bend in the direction of the lead and continue moving forward with momentum.

Change Leads in a Figure Eight

HOW TO

When my horse is changing naturally, I will "train "the lead change. Canter–walk–canter and canter–halt–canter transitions on a figure eight are excellent for this exercise. I like to ride a figure eight as two Ds back-to-back (fig. 9.18 A). However, a figure eight with diagonal lines (fig. 9.18 B) can be useful for practicing flying lead changes if your horse is already well schooled and doesn't fall in as you change direction.

Give yourself a long straight line across the middle or across the diagonal before changing direction to the next circle in the figure eight. Before you slow down to the walk or halt in the center of the figure, begin to flex your horse's head position in the new direction. Make the transition to the walk or halt, and right away back to the new lead at the canter. As you cue for the canter, the horse's hips should move inward on the new circle of the figure eight to complete the bend of his body.

When he is proficient, eliminate the walk or halt in the center of the figure eight. While cantering to the left, flex your horse's head to the right (the new direction coming up) and add right leg contact for bend. Slide your left leg back on the horse's barrel to cue for the right lead, and keep the right rein against the neck. Change leads on the straight line in the middle of the figure eight, *before* you start the new circle at the top or bottom of the figure. After you've completed one figure eight with a lead change, your horse may start to anticipate it, which can work positively in your favor.

COMMON CHALLENGES

☛ *Horse doesn't change leads:* Practice the canter–halt–canter transition. Do not halt for very long. Do this in two stages: First, canter with the horse bent in the direction he is going, then flex the head toward the new lead, halt, and change the bend as you cue for the new lead. Second, canter on the circle and as you make your horse straight in the middle of the figure, flex your horse's head toward the new lead, stay balanced yourself by keeping your shoulders back and pressing downward in the saddle as if you were pushing his hindquarters down, and

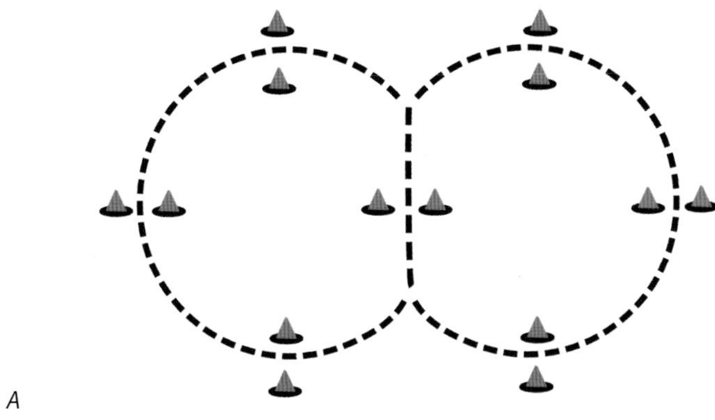

A

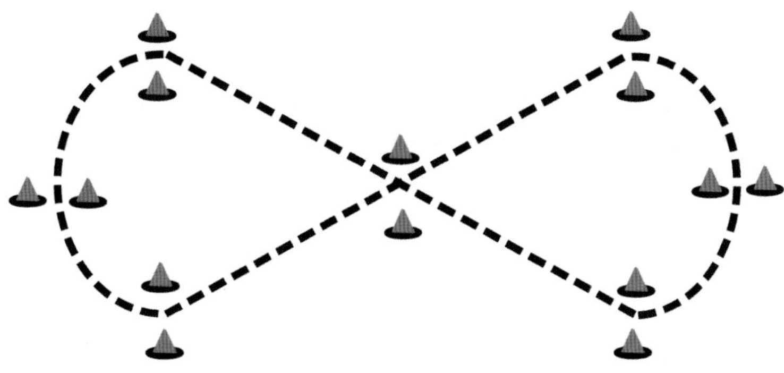

B

▲ *9.18 A & B* A figure eight (A), and a figure eight appropriate for flying lead changes (B).

change the bend as you cue for the new lead. Use cones in the center of the figure eight to test your horse's straightness and balance. When you don't get a change, take a break and start the exercise over the next day.

Change Leads from Yielding

Changing lead from yielding is another great, natural way to encourage a horse to change leads on command. When you have a horse that is yielding well, use this exercise. Yield to the right at the canter with your horse's head already flexed a little to the left, and ask your horse to change lead. Stay straight after the change, as it will help him keep his balance.

For the perfect lead change, both front and hind legs must change leads at the same time. There is one moment as the flying lead change is happening when the horse has all four legs off the ground. If you keep perfecting your walk and halt changes, the horse learns collection during the transitions and the coordination necessary to bring the legs together and lift for the flying change.

An excellent exercise for the horse that commonly changes leads with the front legs then follows with the hind legs is to initiate the change from haunches-out (see p. 158). The horse needs to be able to do haunches-out at the trot with minimum effort and counter-canter well established to do this.

HOW TO

To practice a lead change from right lead to left, start the exercise in a balanced counter-canter. Track to the left on the right lead and proceed with haunches-out at the canter down the long side. Be sure to keep contact with the left indirect rein and leg to straighten the horse and keep the shoulders in line with the hips. When you ask for the change with your right leg, make sure you flex the head left with the left indirect rein and left leg active during the change to keep the horse engaged. When the horse changes lead, continue cantering—now on a diagonal track—and then stop and reward your horse. This exercise really helps the horse to maintain a straight alignment so he is able to change both front and hind legs together during the flying lead change.

COMMON CHALLENGES

☛ *Horse doesn't move laterally and doesn't change lead:* When your horse anticipates this exercise, he may try to go straight and not yield. When you are yielding to the right, use your right indirect rein to slow and straighten the horse to get him yielding properly. When you feel your horse move sideways again, ask for the lead change, and then go straight.

☛ *From haunches-out, horse changes lead in front before behind:* When changing lead from right to left, first check your bend at counter-canter and in haunches-out. Gradually straighten the horse with the left indirect rein, flex the head to the left, and really "turn the key" with your hand to bring more of the rein against the neck. This keeps the horse's shoulder from moving too quickly when you ask for the change. Also, check your position and look ahead to where you are going to ride after the change so you stay centered as the horse changes lead. Try again and again until you get front and hind together. Be patient and your horse will learn on his own.

Change Leads from Counter-Canter

HOW TO

Changing lead from the counter-canter is a natural way to teach it. Ride a circle to the left of sufficient size so your horse can carry his balance easily in his right lead counter-canter. To begin the lead change, flex the horse's head toward the left, his new lead, making sure he stays in straight alignment and doesn't move inward. Your left indirect rein and leg need to be active during the change to keep this alignment on the circle. As you use your right leg to cue for the flying lead change, stay balanced yourself, keep your horse's head flexed toward the new lead, and maintain your horse's straight body alignment on the circle. When your horse does this well, you can advance to changing leads from the correct lead to the counter lead. Success in changing leads in this exercise is all about controlling the horse's body position.

Once you master single flying changes, there is nothing more fun than to learn tempi changes, which are changing lead in a specified sequence of strides. Come and ride with me and I will teach you!

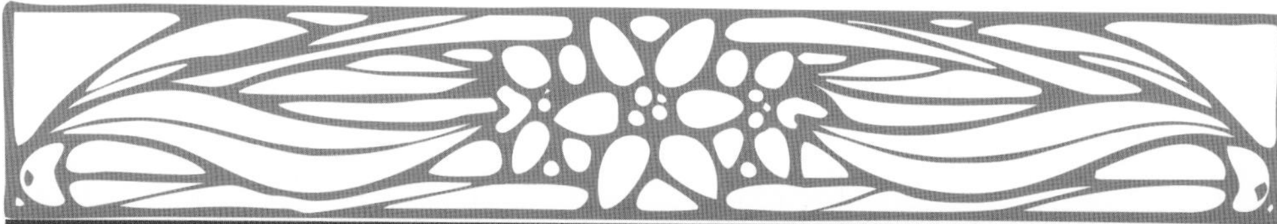

Want More?

If you are looking for more training exercises or figures to practice with your horse, join the United States Dressage Federation (USDF), or study the dressage competition tests, which show beautiful development of horses and riders. There are four tests at every level, and each one is a gradual progression of training the horse to become more collected. It's all right there and as applicable to those who pursue Western sports as those who ride English.

For more than a decade I have worked to develop dressage within my specialty breed, the American Quarter Horse. The year 2010 marks the first time dressage will be officially recognized by the American Quarter Horse Association as they team up with the USDF and the United States Equestrian Federation (USEF). I encourage all stock horse breed owners to get involved in dressage, as it is the perfect way to promote classical, correct horsemanship and secure a happy partnership with your horse!

Do you want to "Ride Well?" At our Palm Partnership Training Clinics, we use dressage to teach you to "Be the rider that your horse deserves!" If you are having difficulty teaching a horse natural collection, I invite you to contact me, as I have many ways to help those of you who are training your own horses at home. Whether you are a professional or an amateur, I love to share my knowledge!

Lynn Palm
www.lynnpalm.com

About Lynn Palm

A pioneer among women in the equine industry, Lynn Palm Pittion-Rossillon has long had a passion for teaching. In fact, she instructed her first clinic in 1970—long before any of her contemporaries considered horsemanship instruction a viable profession. No other clinician today can begin to match Lynn's first-class reputation and proven performance record as an all-around trainer, showman, exhibitor, and entrepreneur.

Some of Lynn's notable accomplishments include: 34 World and Reserve World Championships; Four Superhorse titles; American Quarter Horse Association (AQHA) Female Equestrian of the Year; over 50 bridleless exhibitions with the legendary Rugged Lark at the 1996 Atlanta Olympic Games, National Horse Show, The Washington International, and the International World Cup; 2003 Equine Affair Exceptional Equestrian Educator Award winner; 2006 AQHA Professional Horsewoman of the Year; and the Women's Sports Foundation 2000 Female Equestrian of the Year.

A self-described perfectionist and workaholic, Lynn has built an immensely successful career with a wide spectrum of abilities and experiences. Built upon her foundation in dressage, she has at one time or another studied, competed, exhibited, and/or instructed in the following areas of equestrian sport: dressage, hunter under saddle, Western horsemanship, Western riding, show-

▲ Lynn Palm and My Royal Lark.

manship, English equitation, hunter/jumper, Western pleasure, reining, and working cow horse.

In addition, Lynn has been a staunch advocate of dressage with American Quarter Horses. Her support has been a driving force in getting dressage recognized as an AQHA discipline.

While perhaps best known for her work with two-time Superhorse champion Rugged Lark, Lynn has created a legacy of training and showing an unmatchable cadre of outstanding performance horses. Impressive as her performance record is, Lynn says her primary goal is to educate others on correct riding skills to increase the riding longevity of their horses.

Instead of focusing on helping riders fix *their horses*, Lynn and her husband Cyril Pittion-Rossillon have created Palm Partnership Training with the mission of improving *the rider* first and foremost. The pair conducts Palm Partnership Training courses at Fox Grove Farm in Ocala, Florida, and at Royal Palm Ranch in Bessemer, Michigan. Lynn's "Ride Well" clinics are offered across the country.

Breaking the mold of the old adage, "Those who can't do, teach," Lynn is an all-around Western and English horsewoman and a legend in her own time. From the trails to the show ring, Lynn is "in it to win it" and is a major force in the equine industry as a clinician, competitor, and trainer.

Index

Page numbers in *italics* indicate illustrations.